Praise for Jim O'Coı

GOING THE]

*There is a consoling warmth about this book ... The reflections provide
lasting nourishment for busy, anxious or lonely people.*

Daniel O'Leary

*A silent, gentle book. My hope is that one friend might tell another about
its peace-inducing qualities ... enabling one to face the real world of God
in spite of all the distractions.*

Angela Macnamara

*To those asking: 'Is there any book around, with a bit of Scripture, and
a few thoughts, to help me pray? Something simple. Not too many
words.' Yes, there is, try this one.*

Anne Alcock

*This is a wonderful resource book for anyone who wishes to devote quiet
time to God on a regular basis ... The pages dance with images of God
and God's love.*

Tom Kiggins

*In this book, Fr Jim draws the reader deeply into his own conversation
with the Divine, through the use of a wealth of resources including
prayer, scripture passages, psalms and hymns and many vibrant images
of different kinds. The author contemplates the struggles with which
ordinary people grapple throughout their lives.*

Paul Clayton-Lea

*I was delighted to get and read Fr Jim's book ... In it he invites us to
open our hearts to God in the world around us. The book is divided into
easily manageable sections. I have found reading one of these a helpful
way to calm my mind as part of my night prayer.*

Brian D'Arcy

Invoked or not invoked, God is present.

Carl Jung

Jim O'Connell MHM

A LIFE TO LIVE

AWAKENING TO GOD'S ABIDING PRESENCE

the columba press

First published in 2015 by
the columba press
55A Spruce Avenue, Stillorgan Industrial Park,
Blackrock, Co. Dublin

Cover by RedRattleDesign
Cover image of Dingle Peninsula by Daniel Foley
Origination by The Columba Press
Printed by SprintPrint Ltd

ISBN 978 1 78218 217 7

Appreciation

While the reflections owe much to my own experience down the years, they have also been influenced by what others have written. I am indebted to the following writers that I greatly admire: Daniel O'Leary, Ronald Rolheiser, Liam Lawton, Joan Chittister, Sr Stanislaus 'Stan' Kennedy, Joyce Rupp, Martin Laird, Benignus O'Rourke and the late Henri Nouwen. The writings of these authors (and others of course) have been a help to me on my own journey. You will find echoes of their insights in the reflections.

Three of these people deserve special mention: Daniel O'Leary, Liam Lawton and Sr Stan. They read the reflections prior to publication and you will find Daniel's and Sr Stan's comments on the back cover of the book. I offer sincere thanks to them for agreeing to take on the task and for their support and encouragement. I am especially grateful to Liam Lawton for writing the foreword.

I must also mention those who made a big contribution to the work as it was in progress. Two people in particular painstakingly read an early draft and responded with insights and suggestions that proved very helpful – Noel Keating and my brother, Tim O'Connell. There were others who read the draft and offered me help and encouragement: Maurice McGill, Sr Anne Moore and Donie O'Connor. I must also express my appreciation to Mags Gargan and Jim Flynn for their proofreading skills.

Of course family, friends and Mill Hill colleagues have been very much part of my journey. I am always grateful for their help and support in good times and difficult times along the way. Finally, I thank Patrick O'Donoghue and all at Columba Press.

Table of Contents

Foreword

We live in a world of the immediate. We are constantly evolving and changing. Progress has been so rapid, especially in the last decade, but we are also much more unhappy, dissatisfied and self-absorbed. In the words of our great poet William Butler Yeats: 'We had fed the heart on fantasies, the heart's made brutal by the fare.'

Jim O'Connell recognises this, and in his book offers an antidote to the loneliness that invades the hearts of contemporary men and women – an antidote that is summed up in the quotation from Jean Vanier in chapter seven: 'Open the door of your heart and let this tremendous lover into your being.'[1]

Each chapter offers a unique insight into ordinary themes that are immersed in the mystery that is God. The reader is taken on a journey, like the ancient pilgrim in search of a holy place or indeed a holy face – the face of Christ – which is ultimately revealed in the faces of brothers and sisters who cross our paths.

We are offered personal insights and examples that draw from the wellsprings of Catholic theology and other such sources, giving weight to the human trials and triumphs that the writer experiences in his own quest – trying to fathom and understand the mystery of God becoming one of us: 'And is it true, / This most tremendous tale of all, / Seen in a stained-glass window's hue, / A baby in an ox's stall? / The maker of the stars and sea, / Become a child on earth like me' (John Betjeman).

Jim's experience of the mission fields offers a new landscape which brings the reader face-to-face with a world within a world but always underscored by the challenge of compassion witnessed in the lives of people like Herbert Vaughan and the Mill Hill Missionaries that he founded. Fergal Keane, the BBC correspondent, has had first-hand experience of the work of missionaries around the world and, as we see from his words quoted in chapter six, he was greatly impressed by people such as those that Jim writes about.

A Life to Live is not the biography of a missionary priest, nor does it claim to be, but rather it is a living text of God's abiding presence in the world today that reminds us of the Incarnation – the Word made flesh dwelling among us, but broken for the broken. It is a story without blame, wrapped in mercy. It is a story that is unpopular in a world of revenge and retribution. But, it is a story our world desperately needs to hear and Jim O'Connell, in this book of reflections, witnesses to that story of God made man in Christ – broken for the broken.

Every heart is wounded in some way but with Christ we are offered the chance to be made whole again as the beautiful words of Br Roger remind us in chapter nine, entitled 'Healing a Wounded Heart':

> In every man and in every woman there is a wound, inflicted by failures, humiliations, bad conscience. Perhaps it is caused at a time when we needed infinite understanding and acceptance, and nobody was there to give it … Transfigured by Christ, it is changed into a focus of energy … where communion, friendship and understanding burst forth. (Br Roger of Taize)

A Life to Live will be a companion to the one who seeks to know God and his ways a little more, but especially it will encourage the curious mind that longs to understand the beauty and mystery of God revealed in hidden and unexpected places in our world today. Each chapter enriches our understanding of the Christian call, offering insights into the spiritual life that makes it accessible and inviting to the reader.

The reflections are full of little pearls and gems that will no doubt inspire others as they have inspired me. From Kerry to Kenya there is a breadth of wisdom and insight that comes from an experienced life. I hope these beautiful thoughts and inspirations will help many people (like myself) who struggle to live better and more compassionate lives. The book is so rich and insightful that further comment is not necessary.

Liam Lawton

Introduction

As we rush through life ...

On a cold January morning in 2007, a youngish man entered a metro station in Washington DC and stood near the wall inside the station. He was wearing jeans, a long-sleeved T-shirt and a baseball cap. From a small case, he carefully removed a violin. Placing the open case at his feet, he threw some change into it and began to play.

At a metro station it is not unusual to find a musician performing, but this was a performance with a difference. The musician played six famous pieces of classical music in a performance that lasted around forty-five minutes. During the performance, over one thousand people entered the station, most of them on their way to work. Only seven people stopped and listened for a short while. Among them was one person who recognised the musician and she threw $20 into the case on the ground in front of him. Twenty-six others gave money bringing the total in the open case to $32. The musician finished playing and there was silence. No one noticed and no one applauded. The violinist was Joshua Bell, 'one of the finest classical musicians in the world, playing some of the most elegant music ever written, on one of the most valuable violins ever made'.[2] Two days earlier, he played the same music at a sell-out concert in Boston, where the tickets cost $100.

The Washington Post newspaper had arranged Joshua Bell's performance at the metro station. He was playing a violin that was handcrafted by Antonio Stradivari in 1713. It had been acquired by Bell at a cost that was reported to be in the region of $3.5 million.

What happened in Washington that January morning makes one wonder how much we miss as we rush through life. We are left to ponder the great need to be more reflective and more in tune with the beauty and mystery around us. In the busy hectic lives we live, we can miss the pearl of great price, the treasure hidden in the field of our daily living. Of course people have to work and get things done, but it is unfortunate when too much haste and too much activity close out the deeper aspects of life that are revealed in music, poetry, art, creation, friendship and religious faith. Any or all of these can awaken the heart and help one to engage with mystery – the mystery of God. But it calls for time and effort on our part. St Augustine wrote: 'What calls for all our efforts in this life is the healing of the eye of the heart, with which God is to be seen.'[3]

We may or may not be aware of it as we rush through life, but God is always with us: 'Invoked or not invoked, God is present' (Carl Jung). We have, each of us, a life to live in God's abiding presence. If we are lucky enough to grow up in a loving family, our hearts are awakening to an awareness of this from the beginning. But some of us only come to such awareness in adult life when we awaken to the abiding presence of God in what is there before our eyes in daily life. It can happen suddenly or it can take a lifetime. However long it takes, the God we meet and see is the same God. It does not really matter whether it happens earlier or later in life. This is the lesson of the parable of the workers in the vineyard (Mt 20:1–16). Those who come late receive the same pay, the same reward, as those who had begun work much earlier in the day. This may not be strictly just in our eyes, but it is God's way of doing things; such boundless generosity flows from 'the loving kindness at the heart of our God, who visits us like the dawn from on high' (The Benedictus).

The reflections in this book all explore, in one way or another, the core theme that the eternal God is ever-present with us in the lives we live: 'He is not far from each one of us. For in him we live and move and have our being' (Acts 17:27–8). Each reflection can be seen as a little window that gives a glimpse of the depth of this mystery of our life with God, which ultimately lies beyond our understanding. This is the life to live if we are to satisfy the deepest longings of our human hearts. It is a life that looks towards Jesus: 'Keep your gaze fixed upon Jesus; in him all the anguish and all the longing of the human heart finds fulfilment'

(Pope Francis). In many of the reflections we try to do this – keep our gaze fixed on Jesus. We do it especially in chapter five (the middle chapter of the book) where the seven reflections focus on the Passion, death and Resurrection of Jesus. It is here above all that we see 'the love of God in Christ Jesus our Lord' (Rom 8:39).

Many reflections focus on the heart as the place of the quest and encounter with God, in poverty and in faith.[4] To use St Augustine's image, the quest and encounter involves healing the eye of the heart with which God can be seen. This comes with a spiritual awakening in the human heart as it grows in awareness of a loving God with us and within us. The awakening is a delicate matter that cannot be forced or rushed. We just try to be open to it, receive it in faith and accept it as God's gift. It takes place in hearts that know joy and sorrow, light and darkness. While journeying through these, with a growing awareness of God's abiding presence, we can expect to experience reconciliation, forgiveness, healing, hope and peace.

Since the heart is central to the reflections, we need to be aware that when the word 'heart' is used in the Bible and in Christian writing it means more than it does in ordinary English. Commenting on this, the *New Dictionary of Catholic Spirituality* notes:

> The 'heart' symbolises the centre or core of the human person. It connotes the principle of our personal life, the depth of our integration and insight, the centre of our thinking, feeling and deciding. The word 'heart' defies definition and points beyond itself to mystery.

We try to remember this when the 'heart' comes up in the reflections – as it does so often in phrases such as 'the heart is the place of quest and encounter with God' and 'opening the heart to God's abiding presence and love'.

∽∾

Let the hearts of those who seek the Lord rejoice.
Seek the Lord and his strength;
Seek his presence continually.
(Ps 105:3–4)

CHAPTER ONE

Awakening to God's Abiding Presence

I weave into my life this day the presence of God upon my way.
I weave into the darkest night strands of God all shining bright.
I weave into each deed that's done joy and hope of the Risen Son.
(An Irish prayer)

1.1. Our restless hearts

I have special memories of the swallows. When I was growing up, their coming and going added a fascinating dimension to spring and autumn. My most vivid memories are around their departure in the autumn. As the colours of the leaves changed and fell silently to the ground, the swallows left for warmer shores. All through the summer they had been our constant companions around the farmyard. They built their nests in the hay barn and the other farm buildings. They darted and dived as they swooped and swerved over our heads while we went about our work. Then the weather turned cooler and one day they were there and the next day they were gone. They took something with them. The rafters and roofs of the farm buildings were silent and deserted. The autumn silence was more intense. They were gone to Africa, we were told, and then the greatest miracle of all, in the spring they would return to nest in our barn – the place they had left in the fall of the year. Their slim wings would carry them thousands of miles on the journey to Africa and back.

With the coming and going of the swallows, we learned about migration, which has to be one of nature's greatest and most enduring mysteries. In school and at home we were told that the swallows and other birds travel hazardous journeys of thousands of miles following their own inner radar. They are following an instinct placed in them by their creator. We were also aware of fish, especially salmon, making a journey to the ocean and back to the river to spawn.

Later on, in Africa, I discovered that huge herds of animals also migrate. The distances may be shorter but the migration is equally definite and decisive. Every year around two million animals (mostly wildebeests, zebras and gazelles) migrate in a clockwise rotation covering the Maasai Mara Game Park in Kenya and the Serengeti Park in Tanzania. The herds move south from the Mara to the Serengeti plains in late November and early December. They remain there still moving, following the rains until June or July when the dry season approaches. Then the circle of movement continues back to the greener pastures of the Maasai Mara and the water of the Mara River. The ABC television network in America and a panel of experts declared this annual migration to be one of the 'Seven "New" Wonders of the World'.

It is not surprising that Evelyn Underhill (and others) used the image of migration to describe our journey to God. As she saw it, we have an inner instinct or restlessness that draws us like a magnet deeper and further into the mystery of God. There is a deep desire for God in the human heart – planted there by God. It is like having one's own 'inner radar' – an inner longing, thirst and craving for God that leads to a relentless quest.

The psalmist prayed: 'As a deer longs for flowing streams, so my soul longs for you, O God. My soul thirsts for God, for the living God' (Ps 42). St Augustine summed it up in his prayer: 'You have made us for yourself, O Lord, and our hearts are restless until they rest in you.' St John of the Cross was 'fired with love's urgent longings' as he craved for a union of love with God. He stressed that it is for this we were created and for this we are always hungering: 'The heart is dissatisfied with anything less than God; it was for this goal of love that we were created.' Nothing less than a union of love with God will 'satisfy the heart'.[5]

Old myths and legends express it this way: they tell that before we were born God kissed and caressed our souls.[6] That left a permanent mark, an imprint of a love so deep and pure that we go through life wanting to return to the original experience of such tender love. The memory of God's kiss and caress has created a sacred space deep inside our hearts that is personal and precious. It is the place where our inner instincts, our restlessness, our desire for God are all deeply rooted.

❧

Look into the depths of your heart and ask yourself: do you have a heart that desires something great, or a heart that has been lulled to sleep by things? Has your heart preserved the restlessness of seeking? God awaits you; God seeks you.
(Pope Francis)

1.2. A sense of mystery

When I lived in western Kenya, I spent some time in a rural area called Luanda where I liked to walk in the countryside. One of my favourite walks was along a footpath beside the railway line that ran close to our Mill Hill Formation Centre. The railway track wound its way around the head of a deep fertile valley. There was only one train a day – in the morning. As I walked along the path, I had a view of the magnificent valley. It is a beautiful place, right on the equator. There are lots of little homesteads there, simple structures, some with mud walls and thatched roofs, while others have more permanent brick walls and galvanised roofs. They are very basic and have no electricity or running water. They blend into the landscape and often a maize crop or banana plantation surrounds them. In the glow of the tropical sun in the late afternoon, with the varied shades of light, the valley has a special charm. I found there was a sense of mystery about the place and the people.

The landscape is very much alive with echoes of the past. Time seems to stand still there – with so many reminders of a way of life that has all but disappeared in other parts of the world. People are digging in their gardens (shambas) and carrying water and herding cattle or just sitting outside their homes chatting. They live close to nature and in harmony with creation in the stillness of the valley. In saying this, I am fully aware that there is another side to life for the people there. Behind the silence and serenity there is serious suffering; people live in terrible poverty and frequently get malaria or typhoid and some are infected with the dreaded HIV / AIDS virus.

According to the traditions of the Nuer Tribe in Sudan, the 'Tree where Man was Born' stood in south-western Sudan! Whatever about the tree, there is good reason to believe that humans have been around East Africa for a very long time. Richard Leakey, one of the world's leading experts in these matters, made significant finds of early human remains in north-western Kenya, near Lake Turkana. It was there, at a place called Ileret that Leakey's team discovered what he considers to be some of the earliest human remains – dated at around two hundred thousand years ago. So there may be a whisper of this in the valley – a connection with human history that resonates with the mystery at the heart of nature and human life.

Human history is much more recent in Kerry, nevertheless, I found that the way of life and the valleys and glens of my home area had their own charm and attraction. It was there as a teenage boy that I first became aware of the beauty of God's creation. Despite the hardships of rural life at the time, there were times when I felt a deep sense of peace and solitude. I may not have known it then, but my heart was awakening to the mystery around me. The wisdom from the East tells us that the creator is in creation the way the dancer is in the dance. If you look at the dance, you will see the dancer; if you look at creation, you will see the creator.

There is often a whisper or touch of God that awakens the heart to a sense of mystery in ordinary daily life. Something as familiar as the bread on the table or the water from the tap or the flowers in the garden can be a source of wonder. Just look at a little child; the perfection and fragility of the tiny body at birth can leave one full of awe at such a miracle, while the smile of an infant in its mother's arms tells a story of tender love, security and mystery.

⌘

My beloved, the mountains,
And lonely wooded valleys,
Strange islands and resounding rivers,
The whistling of love-stirring breezes.

The tranquil night
At the time of the rising dawn,
Silent music, sounding solitude.
The supper that refreshes,
and deepens love.[7]

1.3. Watching out for God's presence

During my time in Africa, we had a 'night watchman' where I stayed. He was a local man who came to work, as he called it, when it started to get dark at around seven in the evening and left for home when the dawn broke. He had nights off when a neighbour replaced him. The watchman 'watched' and carried a big stick, a torch and a whistle. He patrolled the property every hour or so and in between his patrols he would sit in a small watchman's hut or on the veranda in front of our house. But even then he would have to be alert to the slightest noise or movement that spelt danger. Fighting sleep was one of his biggest problems and he sometimes lost the battle; now and then we would find him sleeping before we went to bed. If he had taken some of the 'local brew' on his way to work, sleep could come more quickly and snoring was sometimes a problem for him – and for us!

The night must have seemed endless as the watchman kept a long, lonely vigil all through the night waiting for the first signs of dawn. It is not surprising that it was a struggle for him to stay awake and be aware, attentive and alert all the time.

There are similarities between what is required of a good watchman and what helps us on our spiritual journey. We are 'watching' or 'watching out' for God as we struggle to be awake spiritually so that we can notice the various ways in which God is present in us and around us. This is described in the subtitle of this book as: 'Awakening to God's Abiding Presence'. For this to happen alertness is required and attentiveness is essential – as it was for the watchman in his job. In our case it involves 'looking' and 'listening' with the heart, which is greatly helped by having some silence, space and stillness in our day. If we struggle with the need to be active or with weariness and the tendency to doze off (like the watchman), we need not get discouraged but begin again, knowing that God's abiding presence is as certain as the dawn.

When I celebrated my silver jubilee in 1997, I had a small card printed with two short texts from scripture on it. The first text I chose was: 'My presence will go with you, and I will give you rest' (Ex 33:14). Here we have the promise of God's presence – given to Moses and the people of Israel. God himself would go with his people, to be with them at all times: 'In the cloud by day and the pillar of fire by night.' The second text is even more comforting; God is not only with us, God carries us: 'In the wilderness, you saw how the Lord your God carried you, just as one carries a child, all the way you travelled until you reached this place, where you are now' (Deut 1:31).

These texts assure us of God's abiding presence and that God is carrying us along the road we travel as he carried his people long ago. We are living in God's presence, even if we are not aware of it. It is only when we 'watch out' for God and our hearts are touched and awakened that we become aware of God with us and within us. It is not a case of being aware of God in a definite way all the time; it is more like having special occasions when the experience of God is such that it carries us through days and nights when God seems far away or absent.

St Augustine was convinced that the deepest and most intimate encounter with God's abiding presence takes place in the inner self – in the human heart, soul and spirit. He discovered this in his own experience. He felt that before his conversion he had been searching for God in all the wrong places – outside himself. Then came the day when a soft peaceful light streamed into his soul and he awakened to the presence of God in his own heart. He wrote about it later in his *Confessions*: 'You were within me, while I was outside … you were with me but I was not with you.' After many years of searching ('watching out') for God, he found rest at last when he became aware of the one eternal God who had always been present deep in his heart.

❧

In our quest to seek and find God in all things, we must let God search for and encounter us.
(Pope Francis)

1.4. Walk humbly with God

When Moses approached the Burning Bush on Mount Horeb, God said to him: 'Remove the sandals from your feet, for the place on which you are standing is holy ground' (Ex 3:5–6). Moses had to approach the 'burning bush' with a sense of the sacred, a sense of the holy ground on which he was standing. He even covered his face and was afraid to look at God, because he knew he was in God's presence – the infinite, the absolute and eternal mystery.

We can take two images from this story to describe important aspects of our journey into the mystery of God: 'Standing on holy ground' is the image for being in God's presence wherever we are in life. God is found or met where we live our ordinary daily lives, often complicated, confused and sometimes chaotic. 'Take off your shoes' is an image for the humble disposition needed to open our hearts to the mystery of God – with great respect.

Thomas Merton, the mystic and the monk, touches on these images when he describes a contemplative attitude to life, which brings together a humble disposition and the ability to get deep down inside our ordinary experiences to discover what is timeless and eternal there. He wrote:

> It is enough to be in the ordinary human mode, with one's hunger and sleep, one's cold and warmth, rising and going to bed, putting on blankets and taking them off, making coffee and drinking it, defrosting the fridge, reading, meditating … Contemplative prayer is a way of being really inside of our daily experiences. We are in contemplation when we perform the routine tasks of our lives so as to perceive in them that our lives are not little, anonymous or not important any more, but that what's timeless, eternal, is in the ordinariness of things.

For the poet Elizabeth Barrett Browning, ordinary human experience was shot through with the presence of God, but most of the time we fail to see the depths of the mystery before our eyes. She expressed this in her poem *Aurora Leigh*:

> Earth's crammed with heaven,
> And every common bush is afire with God;
> But only he who sees, takes off his shoes,
> The rest sit round it, and pluck blackberries.

'Only he or she who sees takes off his shoes' is a lovely way to describe the need for a humble, prayerful attitude to life that gives one the ability to 'see' with the heart and with respect for the mystery. Such an attitude does not come easily for most of us. Having a humble, reflective, contemplative attitude is very difficult in a culture that is so full of noise and activity. The silence, space and stillness that foster such an attitude are often not part of our day. Unless we take great care, we may not find the opportunity to 'look' and to 'listen' with the heart – to sink down into the waters of life and love that run deep within us and our world. Without some silence and space we can miss the chance to perform the routine tasks in such a way that we can perceive that 'what's timeless and eternal is in the ordinariness of things'. If we 'take off our shoes' and have a humble, respectful, prayerful attitude to life, we will begin to live our lives in God's abiding presence. When we learn 'to walk humbly with your God' (Mic 6:8), we find we are standing on holy ground wherever we are – in touch with the divine in others, in creation and in our own hearts.

❦

God is, and always will be, mystery. Only a non-arguing presence,
only a non-assertive self, can possibly have the humility and honesty to
receive such mysterious silence. When you can remain at peace inside
of your own mysterious silence, you are beginning to receive the immense
'Love that moves the sun and the other stars' – as Dante so beautifully said.
God is always found at the depths, even the depths of our sin and brokenness.
And in the depths, it is silent.
(Richard Rohr, *Sojourners*, March 2013)

1.5. Rooted in the ordinary

Many writers stress the importance of 'finding God in the ordinary' – in the lives we live. For Teresa of Avila, God was present in the kitchen as well as in the chapel. In fact, helping with the washing-up had a special place in her scheme of things; she often recommended it for people who claimed to have visions and revelations. Therese of Lisieux developed the theory of 'the little way', which involved giving full and loving attention to whatever task is at hand, however humble it may be. Ruth Burrows, a Carmelite sister and one of the great spiritual writers of our time, stresses that 'Holiness has to do with the ordinary things.'

Jean Vanier returns time and again to the need to be rooted in the ordinary. In his book *The Broken Body* we read:

> The basis of true human life is a rooting in the earth, faithful relationships, fidelity to those to whom we are bonded in love, carrying one another's burdens, sharing with them their joy and their pain. It is compassion and forgiveness. Small is truly beautiful. Jesus spent thirty gentle loving years with Joseph and Mary, teaching us about being rooted, about a sense of belonging and forming community. Nazareth is our school of life, teaching us to live humbly in the presence of God, to work with our hands, to welcome people as they are, with their gifts and their hurts, to walk in truth, to open our hearts to people and to nature. And in all of this, our model is Joseph, Mary and Jesus in Nazareth. They teach us what it means to be human.[8]

The thirty gentle, loving years that Jesus spent in Nazareth have special significance. For his friends and neighbours, Jesus was simply the son of Joseph and Mary; his true identity as the Son of God was well hidden; nobody suspected anything. Few could believe he was the Messiah, precisely because he was so ordinary, so unlike what people imagined God to be. They were looking for the Messiah, but he did not live up to their expectations. In many ways you could say he was too immersed in the ordinary things we take for granted. He was the carpenter's son from Nazareth and lived like everyone else, in the most ordinary circumstances.[9]

His life in Nazareth is often referred to as 'the Hidden Life' of Jesus – because it was lived in such a quiet and apparently uneventful manner. We find total surprise and wonder later. People were asking about the wisdom that had been granted to him, and they were amazed at the miracles that he worked: 'This is the carpenter's son, surely? Is not his mother the woman called Mary?' (Mt 13:55). They simply saw the son of the carpenter and the child of Mary living an ordinary, even obscure life in which his true identity was hidden.

During his public life, his listeners 'were amazed at the gracious words that came from his mouth' (Lk 4:21). But those lips were silent for thirty years – as far as the public were concerned; there is only one recorded sentence from that period: 'did you not know that I must be about my Father's interests?' (Lk 2:49). Luke pulls back the veil for a few seconds and Jesus then returned to the ordinary daily life at Nazareth, where the stream of love continued to flow between the Father and himself in an outwardly uneventful life. We can learn a lesson from the life in Nazareth; Jesus teaches us to treasure ordinary life as the place to live our lives in God's abiding presence. Holiness is rooted in the ordinary and is open to everybody.

❧

I weave into my life this day, the presence of God upon my way.
I weave into the darkest night, strands of God all shining bright.
I weave into each deed that's done, joy and hope of the Risen Son.
(An Irish prayer)

1.6. A life to live with God

The spiritual writer Carlo Carretto spent much of his life as a hermit in the Sahara desert. He spent his time in silent prayer and translating scripture into the Bedouin language. His writings about prayer, solitude and silence in God's presence have helped many people. In one of his books, there is an interesting reflection about his mother. On one of his visits home it struck him that his mother was a very contemplative, prayerful person – even more than he was. She had an awareness of God's presence deep in her heart, but also in her ordinary daily living. She had spent her life raising a large family, with all the commitment and care that it entailed. She had little chance to spend time alone by herself or in silence with God. She had been so busy and preoccupied over the years, yet she had made great progress in the spiritual life – getting very close to God in the life she lived. This puzzled Carlo at first. He was left to ponder how this could happen without much time for silence and solitude. Then he began to realise that while silence and the desert can help a person come close to God, so too can the demands of family life, responding to the endless needs of children and running a home – as was the case for his mother.[10]

Carlo's mother came close to God, as she opened her heart in unselfish love in ordinary life. God was there in her daily living – in the demands of being a mother, in the situation of having to think of other people's needs before her own. She encountered God in her daily life at home, with its constant outpouring of love for others. His mother's life taught Carlo that in any walk of life, whether one is in the home or in the desert, in the factory or in the fields, when the heart is touched and awakened a person can experience God's abiding presence and be drawn deeply into the mystery of God.

I remember coming upon my father one time as he was sitting on the grass in the middle of one of the high fields of our farm. He was gently smoking his pipe and obviously enjoying the peace and quiet. He was in his seventies then and while doing some light work, he would walk the fields, occasionally stopping to sit down and smoke his pipe. I was near him when he noticed me and before he said anything, I said, 'It is very peaceful.' He thought for a moment and said, 'Yes, you could make your soul here.' I knew what he meant – the silence of the place quietened the mind, calmed the soul and put him in touch with God's presence in that place. Anyone can come to this in the experiences of ordinary life. For the Irish poet Patrick Kavanagh, 'God is in the bits and pieces of every day.'

In a recent interview with *America* magazine, Pope Francis said:

> I see holiness in the patience of the people of God: a woman who is raising children, a man who works to bring home the bread. I see holiness in the sick, in the elderly priests who have so many wounds but have a smile on their faces because they served the Lord, in the sisters who work hard and live a hidden sanctity. This is for me the common sanctity. I often associate sanctity with patience, not only patience to do with the events and circumstances of life, but also as constancy in going forward day by day. This was the sanctity of my parents: my dad, my mom, my grandmother Rosa who loved me so much ... She is a saint who has suffered much, also spiritually, and yet always went forward with courage.

We are all called to holiness; we have a life to live with God. Each person finds his or her way to God when the human heart is awakened to God's abiding presence. It can happen for anyone, in any walk of life, at home or in the desert or anywhere else.

※

St Joseph exercised his role as 'protector' of Jesus and Mary by hearing God's voice and being guided by God's will in his daily life. He did this with fidelity, goodness and tenderness, as a strong and courageous man, a working man, yet in his heart we see great tenderness ...
(Pope Francis)

1.7. Holding God's hand in the darkness

Sharon Commins from Dublin and her companion Hilda Kawuki from Uganda were working for GOAL in Darfur, Sudan, when rebels captured them in July 2009. They were held as hostages for 107 days. It was a terrifying ordeal that was extremely distressing. They were kept out in the open on a mountain, exposed to the heat of the sun by day and barely sheltered from the cold of the night by a light blanket. On a number of occasions they feared for their lives when their captors fired shots over their heads.

When their nightmare came to an end and Sharon was back home in Dublin, she published a message of thanks in the newspapers. She thanked people for their prayers and support and she went on to say:

> Hilda and I sought sanctuary in prayer during our one hundred and seven days in captivity. Prayer gave us the strength to cope with the despair and loneliness on the mountain. Prayer sustained us when virtually all hope was gone and protected us from the crippling fear and deep sadness. Every morning we prayed for the strength and courage to get through the hours. We knew the God we shared would help reunite us safely with our families ... Before settling in to sleep, we prayed that guardian angels would remain with us throughout the night and watch over us until daylight. We are both safe today – and I have no doubt in my mind that our combined prayers made a difference.

Through all the darkness and distress, hardship and loneliness, Sharon and Hilda found solace in prayer and believed that God would help reunite them safely with their families. They managed to hold on to glimmers of hope in their darkest hours of anguish and fear.

We can also recall the experience of Brian Keenan and John McCarthy who were held captive in Beirut for five years by Muslim extremists. Brian wrote that during their dreadful ordeal:

> At times God seemed so real and so intimately close. We talked not of a God in the Christian tradition but of some force more primitive, more immediate and more vital, a presence rather than a set of beliefs ... In its own way our isolation had expanded the heart not to reach out to a detached God, but to find and become part of whatever God may be.[11]

Fortunately, few people have to endure the terrifying experience of being held in captivity by rebels or extremists, but many people endure great hardship and suffering in their ordinary lives. If they are blessed with an awareness of God, they are able to go on hoping that no matter how bleak things are, God will bring them through in the end. Our parents and grandparents were a good example of this. They lived through very difficult times, yet they managed to maintain a positive outlook on life. There were plenty of reasons to be worried and fearful, but they did not allow things to overwhelm them. They were convinced that there was something beyond their problems that was more enduring and important. This conviction was rooted in faith and nourished in prayer. They had strength of spirit, heart and soul that was grounded in humble faith in God's abiding presence and providence. It served them well. They were in touch with the divine and this brought hope in the dark and difficult times: 'Lord, if I hold your hand in the darkness, it is enough.'

In the aftermath of the Celtic Tiger, we are living in troubled and difficult times. Many people have lost their jobs, some have lost their homes and pensions, while others have lost their savings, and nearly everybody has been affected in some way by the levies and cutbacks. Tens of thousands of young people have emigrated, leaving lonely parents behind.

These are testing times for young and old alike. We pray for deeper trust in God who is with us in our trials and troubles – always present in the darkness and difficulties that many of us encounter in our daily lives.

❧

Lord, if I hold your hand in the darkness, it is enough …
Since I know that although I stumble as I go, you do not fall.
(Old Irish prayer)

CHAPTER TWO

Divine Love Embraces Us

Your divine love is a love that clothes us,
enfolds and embraces us,
and completely surrounds us, never to leave us.
(Julian of Norwich)

May God enfold us in the mantle of his love.
(Irish blessing)

2.1. In God's embrace

In July 1986, the spiritual writer Henri Nouwen visited the Hermitage Gallery in St Petersburg to see Rembrandt's painting, *The Return of the Prodigal Son*.[12] He was deeply moved by the experience. The beauty and colours of the painting stunned him. But most of all he was touched by 'the light-enveloped embrace of father and son surrounded by four mysterious bystanders'. He spent a number of hours meditating on the painting and as the evening drew near the 'embrace of father and son became deeper and deeper, and the bystanders participated more directly in the mysterious event of reconciliation, forgiveness, and inner healing'. In the years that followed, the painting was very important for Henri Nouwen's own journey and for his writings. He came to see it as containing 'the heart of the story that God wants to tell ... all of the Gospel is there'.

I have a print of the painting and I can see that one cannot but be touched by Rembrandt's depiction of the father embracing his son. He welcomes him home with a humble gesture of love, bending forward as he holds him in a gentle embrace. The son is quietly kneeling in front of his father, resting against him. He does not seem to be concerned about the resentful stare of his older brother on the right, nor about the other people in the background, who are observing the moving encounter. He looks at peace as his heart is deeply touched by the warmth of his father's welcome.

The parable of the prodigal son (Lk 15:11–32) is a central parable in the teaching of Jesus. Rembrandt's painting focuses on the part of the parable that portrays the father's welcome for the prodigal son. But we must also remember the later part of the story that focuses on the prodigal's older brother, the righteous one, who was upset and resentful. The father who embraced the younger son is also patient and gentle with the older son: 'Son, you are always with me, and all I have is yours.'

The parable and the painting emphasise that God is a merciful father who embraces all – whether one travels the road of the prodigal or remains at home like his resentful, righteous brother. God welcomes everyone in such a way that we can expect our hearts to be touched and awakened by the experience of his love and mercy.

The words 'mercy' and 'embrace' are frequently on the lips of Pope Francis. In one of his first homilies after he became pope, he said:

> The face of God is that of a merciful father who is always patient with us ... It is not easy to trust oneself to the mercy of God, because His mercy is an unfathomable abyss – but we must do it. God has the ability to forget ... He kisses you, He embraces you.

At the World Youth Day 2013 in Rio de Janeiro, Francis addressed a gathering of around three million young people and invited them to join him at Mass 'to meet Jesus, and feel the warmth of his mercy and his love'. The previous day he had said: 'I am here to meet young people coming from all over the world, drawn to the open arms of Christ the Redeemer.'

In God's embrace the human heart is touched and awakened. The word 'embrace' is important. It suggests that God reaches out to us in love and that we are never alone or beyond God's reach. God is a merciful Father whose presence is an active, loving presence. This is illustrated in the painting, emphasised by the parable and stressed by Pope Francis in his homilies.

❧

The face of God is that of a merciful father who is always patient with us.

Let us never lose trust in the patience and mercy of God.
(Pope Francis)

2.2. 'God is love'

There is a story about a child who was drawing a picture and her mother asked her what she was doing. The child replied, 'I am drawing a picture of God.' Her mother said, 'How can you do that, no one knows what God looks like?' 'They will when I finish my picture,' the child replied, as she continued with her drawing. The child had her own version of what God looked like! In a sense, each person has his or her own picture of God. And the picture or image that we have of God has a deep effect on us and on the way we live our lives. The way we see God, or imagine what God is like, can help us or hinder us in the life of faith.

There is a story told by Ronald Rolheiser that can give us a good picture of God:

> A mother is looking out through a window, standing behind a chair, waiting for her daughter and son to get off the school bus at the end of the drive. The little girl comes first, her hair flying free, her laces undone, her books slipping from under her arm. Trying to race her to the front door, the boy's tie is hanging loose, his socks are down around his ankles, his shirt sticking out. The mother leans forward on the back of the chair so that she can keep them both in view for as long as possible; something tells her she mustn't miss this moment, as she is aware of the love and delight that is welling up in her heart.

This story gives us a good image of God and insights into the nature of God. We can picture God looking at us and loving us with great delight. And God is looking at us, not from a distance, as the song says, but from very close to us, for God is always near us, with us and in us. God is with us lovingly and holding us in a loving embrace. We are children of a loving God. Our God is like the loving mother in the story – watching her children with waves of love welling up in her heart.

This is the picture of God that we find in Pope Benedict's encyclical, *Deus Caritas Est* (God is Love). The letter begins with the text of scripture: 'God is Love, and those who abide in love abide in God, and God abides in them' (1 Jn 4:16). Pope Benedict comments that this text expresses with 'remarkable clarity the heart of the Christian faith':

It gives us the Christian image of God and the resulting image of mankind and its destiny ... In the same verse, Saint John offers a kind of summary of the Christian life in these words: 'We have come to know and believe in the love God has for us.' We have come to believe in God's love: in these words the Christian can express the fundamental decision of his or her life ...

Being Christian is ... the encounter with an event, a person, which gives life a new horizon and a decisive direction. St John's Gospel [Jn 3:16] describes the event in these words: 'God loved the world so much that He sent His only Begotten Son, so that everyone who believes in Him may have eternal life.'

Jesus, God's only son, reveals the love of God, the heart of God, the care of God and the face of God. We can come to know this God, who reaches out to us wanting to heal and comfort us. We often find it difficult to believe this and to reach this kind of experience. There are many difficulties along the way. To believe in a loving God, a God who is love itself, does not come easily. Yet, we are assured that God is love and that the spiritual journey is the story of the human heart awakening to the mystery of this loving God, whose 'divine love clothes us and enfolds us, never to leave us'.

❦

The whole meaning of our existence and the one consuming desire of the heart of God is that we let ourselves be loved.
(Ruth Burrows)

2.3. A loving God with us – humbly and gently

Some years ago I watched a television programme on the origins of the Pyramids in Egypt. The programme claimed that the Pyramids have their origins in the religious beliefs of the ancient Egyptians. These beliefs were very much focused on the stars and the heavens. The idea was that they would 'create heaven on earth' by reproducing the pattern of the stars and the heavens. The three Great Pyramids are designed to reproduce the pattern of the constellation Orion. The programme contained some marvellous shots of the sky at night; being taken in the desert made them all the more impressive.

As I watched them, they brought me back to my early days. We often gazed into that same sky when we travelled at night. We had the experience of watching the stars and felt the stillness, the silence and the solitude of the night. It was all there, long before we knew much else about the universe. We did not know that the stars nearest to us are so far away that light travelling from them at the speed of 186,000 miles per second takes more than four years to reach us. And the stars furthest away, but still visible to us, are so distant that light travelling at the same speed takes eight hundred years to get here!

We were children of the universe, though we did not see it that way at the time. Much later the realisation dawned that this experience opened us to infinity, eternity, mystery. Consider that there are perhaps billions of galaxies, with trillions of light years separating them and that at the centre of it all there is the infinite and eternal God who is the creator and sustainer of all life and watches over and cares for every person and every thing. 'No hair falls from a human head nor a sparrow from the sky,' without God knowing and deeply caring. God holds everything in a loving embrace. And that is not all.

We believe that this caring, loving God, this centre of everything, is with us humbly and tenderly. Our God was carried for nine months in the womb of Mary and was born into our world as the child Jesus. The scene depicted by the crib, and the child at the centre of it, is the way God chose to come to us. We cannot understand this great mystery of the Incarnation and words fail us when we try to express it. All we can do is believe that the child in the manger is Immanuel – God with us (Mt 1:23). This is the 'Good News' – the consoling warmth of God's love takes on human form and is now ours to experience and share with others.

This 'Good News' of the Incarnation does not save us from suffering and distress in this life, but it can help us to see some meaning in it. In the words of Avery Dulles:

> The Incarnation does not mean God saves us from the pains of this life. It means that God-is-with-us. For the Christian, just as for everyone else, there will be cold, lonely seasons, seasons of sickness, seasons of frustration, and a season within which we will die. The Incarnation does not give us a ladder to climb out of human life and the human condition. It gives us a drill that lets us burrow into the heart of everything that is, and there find it shimmering with divinity.

In Jesus, 'God is with us' humbly and gently at the heart of everything that is, so that we can find it shimmering with divinity. This is the mystery of the Incarnation, when God clothes us and enfolds us with divine love, so that we can now continue to make Jesus present in the world today through our humility, gentleness and kindness – through our love of God and neighbour.

∽

May the God of gentleness be with you, caressing you with sunlight, rain and wind. May his tenderness shine through you to warm all who are hurt and lonely. May the blessing of gentleness be upon you.
(An Irish blessing)

2.4. 'Now, I too am one of you'

In the second half of the nineteenth century, a Belgian priest, Fr Damien, chose to work with the lepers on the island of Molokoi. It was a very brave thing to do. He knew that he could never again leave the island, and that he would inevitably get leprosy himself. Miraculously, Damien worked with the lepers for twelve years before he got leprosy. Then one night, when he was washing his feet, he found he had lost the feeling in his right foot – the first sign that he had contracted the disease. The following Sunday he began his sermon with the words: 'Now, I too am one of you.' He felt he had now identified with the lepers in their dreadful condition. Fr Damien was canonised in October 2009 and is now St Damien.

We can take the little phrase 'Now, I too am one of you,' and imagine it on the lips of Jesus. Jesus is God and man and one of us. Jesus identifies with us in our humanity, in our suffering and our weakness and died for us out of love. Though he was sinless he took our sins on Himself. He is with us at the heart of life – in human flesh and blood. He is our King: 'The King is Jesus; in him God entered humanity and espoused it to himself' (Pope Benedict XVI).

The words 'king' and 'kingdom' may not be among our favourite words, but they are used in the New Testament with a special meaning. Jesus is a 'king' who is with us – loving and serving and redeeming us, and his 'kingdom' is about love, mercy, justice, joy, compassion and peace: 'The kingdom of God is not food and drink, but righteousness and peace and joy in the Holy Spirit … Let us then pursue what makes for peace and mutual upbuilding' (Rom 14:17–19).

'The kingdom of God is here' were the first words that Jesus spoke when he began his preaching – as recorded in St Mark's Gospel. In Jesus himself, the kingdom of God is here – the love and mercy of God is being made manifest in him and in our hearts, our lives and our world – renewing and reconciling all things.

The nineteenth-century Danish sculptor Thorvaldsen made a clay model for a statue of Christ, his arms raised in triumph and glory. But the weight of the soft clay was too much for the inner structure and in the morning, when he entered his studio he saw the arms had sagged downwards. At first he felt deeply disappointed, but when he examined it carefully he saw that it now expressed something deeper than the triumph and glory that he had intended the previous evening. It now expressed welcome, compassion, and forgiveness. It portrayed a humble Christ, in whom the kingdom of God is here, the compassion of God is here, the forgiveness of God is here, the peace of God is here, the welcome and embrace of God is here – where we live our lives now.

Jesus Christ is now one of us, present in our hearts and in our world. When our hearts are awakened to his presence, 'divine love clothes us, enfolds us and embraces us and completely surrounds us, never to leave us'.

A final thought here: there is always movement from the presence of divine love (God's kingdom) in our hearts and lives to concrete, living, loving action, expressing itself in compassion, forgiveness and loving service. In Christian living, love and action belong together, faith and life merge. Mother Teresa summed it up as follows: 'The fruit of Silence is Prayer. The fruit of Prayer is Faith. The fruit of Faith is Love. The fruit of Love is Service. The fruit of Service is Peace.'

∞

Spread love everywhere you go: first of all in your own house ... Let no one ever come to you without leaving better and happier. Be the living expression of God's kindness – kindness in your face, kindness in your eyes, kindness in your smile, kindness in your warm greeting.
(Blessed Teresa of Calcutta)

2.5. The power of love

When the late Cardinal Basil Hume delivered the DeLubac Lecture in 1998, he talked about the power of love and he quoted from the writings of Viktor Frankl who was imprisoned in Auschwitz concentration camp. Viktor's wife was also a prisoner at a neighbouring camp but they were not allowed to see each other. Viktor described how he was stumbling to work with a group of prisoners in the icy wind before dawn, driven by guards using rifle butts. Suddenly, his loving wife entered his mind and he had an experience that brought profound insights into the power of love:

> Real or not, her look was then more luminous than the sun which was beginning to rise. A thought transfixed me; for the first time in my life I saw the truth as it is set into song by so many poets and proclaimed as the final wisdom by so many thinkers: that love is the ultimate and the highest goal to which we can aspire. I grasped the meaning of the greatest secret that human poetry and human thought have to impart: the salvation of man is through love and in love. I understood how a man who has nothing left in the world may still know bliss – in utter desolation. When he cannot express himself in positive action, when his only achievement may consist in enduring his suffering in the right way, man can still achieve fulfilment.

These words of Viktor Frankl came from the heart of utter desolation: 'A man who has nothing left in the world may still know bliss – in utter desolation!' We are not likely to experience that level of desolation or even experience the same depth of love, but as soon as we begin to experience the power of love in our hearts, we can expect great things to happen for us, even if our 'only achievement consists in enduring suffering in the right way'.

Some people grow bitter and resentful when they encounter suffering while others experience the power of love in and through suffering. In humble faith, they grow close to God and experience his loving presence. This is not something superficial, soft or sentimental. Their knowledge of a loving God comes from a deep experience of God's closeness to them. Richard Rohr says that great love and great suffering are the pathways into this kind of experience. People travel these pathways in their daily encounters with good and evil, darkness and light, sorrow and sickness – experienced in their own lives and the lives of others. While they are well aware of the darkness and difficulties, like Viktor Frankl, they manage to believe in the power of love that clothes them and enfolds them.

There is a short verse of scripture in St John's Gospel that is relevant here. It expresses the most profound truth of our faith. It comes from the lips of Jesus: 'The Father himself loves you, because you have loved me and believe that I came from God' (Jn 16:27). This is the unique revelation that Jesus gives us. The Father loves us and Jesus is the revelation of that love. If we believe in Jesus and love Him, we can find our way into a deep experience of the Father's love, the Father's embrace. Jesus is the way to the Father's heart and house. He loves us with an everlasting love and it is the power of this divine love that sustains us on our journey. We are called to accept that love, to live it in daily life and to share it by loving others and all God's creation. When we manage to do this, however imperfectly, we realise, like Viktor Frankl, that our 'salvation ... is through love and in love'.

Love people even in their sin, for that is the semblance of divine love and is the highest love on earth. Have no fear of human sin. Love all God's creation, the whole of it and every grain of sand in it. Love every leaf, every ray of God's light. Love the animals, love the plants, and love everything. If you love everything, you will begin to comprehend it better every day, and you will come at last to love the world, always, with an all-embracing love.
(Fyodor Dostoyevsky, *The Brothers Karamazov*)

2.6. God's abiding love and mercy

In one of his homilies, Pope Francis told a story of a widow who came to him after a Mass for the sick when he was Archbishop of Buenos Aires: 'An elderly lady approached me for confession – humble she was, so very humble, more than eighty years old. I looked at her, and said, "Grandmother," (where I come from, we call the elderly grandmother and grandfather) "Would you like to make your confession?" "Yes," she said, and I said, "But, if you have not sinned", and she said, "We all have sinned". I replied: "If God should not forgive you?" and she replied, "The Lord forgives everything". I asked, "How do you know this for sure?" and she replied, "If the Lord hadn't forgiven all, then the world wouldn't still be here."' The Pope went on to say: 'Here we have wisdom that the Holy Spirit gives, interior wisdom regarding the mercy of God.'

This is one of the many occasions that Pope Francis has spoken about the love and mercy of God since he became pope. In the homily that he preached on Divine Mercy, Sunday 2013 (2nd Sunday of Easter), he spoke about God's love, mercy, tenderness, patience, forgiveness, God's 'embrace' and 'caress of love'. He began: 'What a beautiful truth of faith this is for our lives: the mercy of God! God's love for us is so great, so deep; it is an unfailing love, one which always takes us by the hand and supports us, lifts us up and leads us on.'

He gave the example of the two disciples on the road to Emmaus:

> Their sad faces, their barren journey, their despair. But Jesus does not abandon them: he walks beside them and patiently explains the scriptures which spoke of himself, and he stays to share a meal with them. This is God's way of doing things. He is not impatient like us. God is patient with us because he loves us, and those who love are able to understand, to hope, to inspire confidence; they do not give up, they do not burn bridges, they are able to forgive.

He said that the parable of the prodigal son always gives him great hope:

The father – had he forgotten the son? – No, never. He is there, he was waiting for him every hour of every day; the son was always in his father's heart ... The father, with patience, love, hope and mercy, had never for a second stopped thinking about him, and as soon as he sees him still far off, he runs out to meet him and embraces him with tenderness, the tenderness of God, without a word of reproach. In that embrace is the joy of the father.

Referring to Thomas the Apostle he said:

With patience: Jesus does not abandon Thomas in his stubborn unbelief; he gives him time, he does not close the door, he waits. With the words: 'My Lord and my God', Thomas lets himself be enveloped by divine mercy; he sees it before his eyes in the wounds of Christ's hands and feet and in his open side, and he discovers trust; he is a new man, no longer an unbeliever but a believer.

And this is what he said about Peter the Apostle:

Peter feels the loving gaze of Jesus and he weeps. How beautiful is this gaze of Jesus – how much tenderness is there? Let us never lose trust in the patience and mercy of God ... God is always waiting for us: he never grows tired. Jesus shows us this merciful patience of God so that we can regain confidence and hope – always! I would like to emphasise one other thing: God's patience calls forth in us the courage to return to him, however many mistakes and sins there may be in our life.

Pope Francis offers us deep insights into God's abiding love and mercy – the 'divine love that clothes us, enfolds and embraces us, and completely surrounds us, never to leave us'.

Let us find the courage to return to God's house, allowing ourselves to be loved by him and to encounter his mercy in the sacraments. We will feel his wonderful tenderness, we will feel his embrace, and we too will become more capable of mercy, patience, forgiveness and love.
(Pope Francis)

2.7. Loving God deliver us from evil

A weekend in September 2013 brought some very distressing news. It started with the El Shabab terrorist attack on the Westgate Shopping Centre in Nairobi that left nearly a hundred people dead and hundreds more injured. Then came the news of two suicide bombers killing nearly one hundred people leaving a church after Mass in Peshawar, Pakistan. Subsequently there was news of a suicide bomber killing more than a hundred people at a funeral in Iraq. That same weekend we heard about a group of innocent people being killed in Afghanistan by American drones that are supposed to target terrorists. In all these dreadful incidents, the dead were innocent people (men, women and children) going about their daily lives – shopping, going to church and attending a funeral. Nearer home, there were two murders in Dublin over that weekend, victims of the ongoing gang violence that it is part of life in so many cities. The frequency of these dreadful atrocities is a stark reminder of the presence of evil in the world.

Thomas Moore and Robert L. Moore are two well-known American writers whose books on spirituality are widely read. Their writings often focus on the presence of good (God) and evil (the Devil). They differ significantly in the way they approach and deal with the subject. Robert Moore himself quotes what another writer, Thomas Brunner, said about this: 'While Thomas Moore's books may be sifted down into the maxim "the sacred is closer than you think", Robert Moore's books exhibit the central idea that "the demonic [the Devil, evil] is closer than you think".'[13] Responding to this comment, Robert Moore says that this description of his work misses some of the more subtle connections that he sees between the sacred (good) and evil. But it does grasp the urgency of his concern that we all need to wake up to a better understanding of 'the great solar fires that operate unconsciously within us to drive the increasing epidemics of personal and social evil'. These epidemics lead to the violence and wars around the world.

Over the years, I have been more inclined towards the line taken by Thomas Moore – that the sacred (God) is closer than we think. Indeed, many of the reflections in this book focus on the presence of God and goodness in our lives and world. But we cannot but be aware of the presence of evil in our midst. As time passes, I have been taking more seriously Robert Moore's emphasis that evil is closer than we think. Both maxims taken together give us a more complete picture. Good and evil are both nearer than we think – a reality in our hearts and world.

The Cherokee Indians sum it up in the following story about a battle that goes on inside us – a battle between two 'wolves'. One is a bad wolf – seen in anger, envy, jealousy, greed, guilt, resentment, lies, arrogance and pride. The other wolf is good – seen in joy, peace, love, hope, serenity, humility, kindness, generosity, truth, compassion and faith. To the question: which wolf wins? – The answer is simple: The one you feed. This story highlights the struggle going on in our hearts between good and evil. They are both closer than we think.

On the journey of faith, we try to feed the good wolf and be delivered from the bad one. Every time we pray the 'Our Father' we ask our loving God to 'deliver us from evil' – the evil one.

Pope Francis often speaks about evil and the Devil. He sees the temptations of the evil one in everyday life, in something as commonplace as gossip. He also emphasises that through the Spirit of our loving God we can be delivered from evil and be born into a new life that is meek and charitable.

❧

When we prefer to gossip, gossip about others, criticise others – these are everyday things that happen to everyone, including me – these are the 'temptations of the evil one', who does not want the Spirit to come to us and bring about peace and meekness in the Christian community. These struggles always exist in the parish, in the family, among friends. Through the Spirit we are born into a new life that is meek and charitable.
(Pope Francis)

CHAPTER THREE

'The Heart is the Place'

*The heart is the place of the quest and
encounter – in poverty and in faith.*[14]

The mystery enters through the heart.
(Pope Francis)

3.1. Their hearts were thrown open[15]

The Shawshank Redemption is a film about life in a maximum security prison in the United States. It is a story of hardship and hope, of friendship and survival, within the prison walls. It is a story about the triumph of the human spirit in the most adverse surroundings. There are some harsh scenes in the film, but there are many moving moments.

City banker, Andy Dufresne, arrived in Shawshank prison in 1947, convicted of two brutal murders. He had received a double life sentence yet, later in the film, the revelations of a new prisoner confirmed Andy's innocence.

Within the confines of the prison, Andy formed a friendship with the prison 'fixer' and became popular with the prison guards. He also earned the respect of the warden, so he was given some of the more responsible jobs, including a job in the library which he had helped establish. One day, some boxes of books and old records were delivered. When he was going through the records, Andy found a record that he fancied. While the prison guard was in the toilet, Andy locked the toilet and library doors. He then placed the record on the player, switched on the prison public address system, and in a short time the whole prison compound was filled with the beautiful music of a love song from Mozart's *The Marriage of Figaro*. The result was dramatic. All over the prison yard, the prisoners stopped work and raised their heads, as their hearts were thrown open by to the sound of the music and the love song being sung by the two singers. The narrator said that, 'Those two voices were singing about something so beautiful that it cannot be expressed in words, higher than anybody in this dead place dares to dream. It was like some beautiful bird descended into our drab little cage, making those hard black walls dissolve away – and for the briefest moment every last man at Shawshank felt free.'

Andy was sent to the 'hole' for two weeks, as punishment. When he returned to his mates, he told them that he had Mozart with him in that awful place. Pointing to his heart, he said, 'It is there; they cannot take it from me.' In very different circumstances, William Wordsworth, the great English poet, described a similar experience in these words: 'The music in my heart I bore, long after it was heard no more.' As the film presents it, the music and the love song touched the hearts of the hardened prisoners. For a brief interval, their hearts were thrown open and they were swept away into another world. They felt free, despite the dark walls that surrounded them. Their cruel grim world was transformed for a few minutes.

The prisoners got a fleeting glimpse of something deeper. They may have got a taste of the mystery of love that can be part of all our lives. This kind of experience is open to everyone when the heart is thrown open. For some people, it may just be something passing, while for others it can be the beginning of something deep, rich and lasting – a spark that ignites love in the heart and sets one on the road to change for the better. This can be a long journey. As St Augustine and so many others discovered, a life-transforming experience has to be lived out in a 'change of heart' that manifests itself in love and compassion, in forgiveness and humility, in hope and gratitude. This comes about when the heart is touched and awakened by an experience of God's abiding love. It can change a person's life forever.

❦

As big soft buffetings come at the car sideways
And catch the heart off guard and blow it open.
(Seamus Heaney, 'Postscripts')

3.2. 'The heart is the place'

In Christian writings, the 'heart' usually indicates the centre of the personality – the source of life, love, knowledge, dispositions and attitudes. The word 'heart' occurs over a thousand times in the Bible. According to McKenzie's *Dictionary of the Bible*, the word 'heart' means even more in Hebrew than it does in English. In Hebrew it signifies the entire inner life of a person and it is normally used in this sense in the Christian tradition. This is the context in which we understand the word 'heart' in the quotation from the Catechism: 'The heart is the place of this quest and encounter, in poverty and in faith.' The heart is home to God's abiding love and presence: 'The love of God has been poured into our hearts by the Holy Spirit which has been given to us' (Rom 5:5).

There is a curious little story about God's presence in the human heart that Anthony de Mello used to tell:

> God was feeling tired of people pestering him and needed to take a holiday. In trying to decide where to go to get away from people, he turned to the angels for advice. One angel suggested he should go to the top of the highest mountain on earth, but the other angels felt that was not a great idea, since people climb that mountain regularly these days. Another felt he should go to the depths of the sea, but again that was rejected because people would find him there. Another suggestion was to go and hide on the far side of the moon but human beings are now going to the moon. Then a wise and trusted angel said quietly: Go and hide in the human heart – people will never dream of searching for you there.

As de Mello noted, the story comes from someone with a good imagination, but it conveys a very important message about God's presence within us. People often travel long distances seeking God and searching for God in all sorts of places, while they are unaware of God with them and within them – in their own hearts.

When St Augustine found that God was present in his heart, he looked back with regret: 'You were there before my eyes, but I had deserted even my own self, and I did not find the God of my own heart.' We can also hear his plea: 'Come back to your heart, in your inner self Christ has made his home.'

With the abiding presence of God in the human heart, we are deep into mystery. We need not be surprised if we find it difficult to grasp, experience and express. At least, we can begin with the belief that the heart is the place of our quest for God and encounter with God – in poverty and faith. When we come to accept this and start to experience it for ourselves, however imperfectly, we take an important step on our journey into the mystery of God. Rather than trying too hard, we move into the area of 'awareness' and 'awakening' and 'allowing'.

It is a great blessing when our hearts awaken to the mystery of God within us and around us. It is like waking up from sleep – moving from being asleep to being awake spiritually. We allow the God who has always been present with us to come into our awareness warmly and quietly. This brings a deep sense of presence: 'How gently and lovingly you wake in my heart, where in secret you dwell alone. And in your sweet breathing, filled with good and glory, how tenderly you swell my heart with love' (St John of the Cross: *The Living Flame of Love*).

We may wonder why it is that we cannot be more in touch with God's loving presence in our hearts. This is the way one writer sees it:

> We haven't looked at ourselves with the merciful, tender, compassionate eyes of God. So we walk in despair half the time. As a result, the ability to realise that God is in our midst and in us – a realisation that is the fruit of faith – fades and disappears.[16]

⸙

One can always enter into inner prayer, independently of conditions of health, work or emotional state. The heart is the place of this quest and encounter, in poverty and in faith.
(CCC 2710)

3.3. Going the heart's way to God

John Moriarty from Moyvane, Co. Kerry, was an extraordinary man. Sadly, he passed away in 2007. He was a philosopher, storyteller, writer and mystic. Images and symbols, metaphors and myths, together with creation and the world of nature, are all central to his writings. He spent much of his life in search of wisdom and trying to understand the universe. At one stage, he turned his back on Christianity but later returned to it with great energy and enthusiasm. His search took him to various parts of the world. He studied literature and mythology from many cultures and he was never satisfied with what he found, however interesting it was. The answers coming from science left him particularly disappointed.

John taught English literature for seven years at the University of Manitoba in Canada, but gave up his post to return to Ireland and settle in Connemara, where he lived the simple life for seventeen years before returning to his native Kerry. It was during that time in Connemara that he 'reconnected with his soul'. He could spend hours sitting by a waterfall in total silence under the Maamturk mountains and was deeply moved by what he experienced in the glens and woods. He meditated outside of books, and after a great deal of it, saw fit to return to 'his mother tongue, Christianity'.

So his experiences in Connemara helped him to reconnect with his heart and soul and find his way back to Christianity, which he came to value and appreciate in a new way. He wrote these lines a couple of years before he died:

> Unlike so many Romantic poets, I couldn't be content with the natural liturgy of lake water lapping, or with the natural sounds, just sounds, of linnets' wings. The truth is, I once was. Indeed, for three years in Connemara I was rapturously content with them ... But then there was a day when it only took one small lap of Loch Inagh water and not only were the mirrored mountains gone, the world was gone and I was in a void that I didn't immediately or soon afterwards recognise to be God in His enduring mode as Divine Mirum [wonder, miracle, mystery].[17]

In later life, John's Christian faith (his mother tongue, as he described it) played a big part in leading him to go the heart's way (soul's way) into the mystery of God. The sacraments helped him and sheltered him on his way:

> The thing about sacraments and rituals is that while it is the intention of many of them to bring us into contact with God, they simultaneously shelter us against what might otherwise be an un-insulated and therefore wholly incinerating encounter with God … Such are the Christian sacraments, a safe or at the very least a safer way of drawing nigh unto God.[18]

He spent his later years helping others to find their way. He conducted retreats for large groups of people and gave lectures that were helpful to many. He had a wonderful way with telling stories and weaving the wisdom he had gleaned over the years into these stories that were often drawn from his experience of growing up in north Kerry. He led many people along the soul's way, the heart's way – the Christian way – into the mystery of divine love that enfolds us all. John knew that 'The heart is the place of the quest and encounter, in poverty and in faith.' He himself had discovered how true this is and helped others in their quest for and encounter with God.

⌘

> *Clear days bring the mountains right down to my doorstep,*
> *Calm nights give the rivers their say,*
> *The wind puts its hand to my shoulder some evenings,*
> *And then I don't think,*
> *I just leave what I am doing and I go the soul's way.*[19]

> *'Where then do we begin?' Meister Eckhart was asked.*
> *His answer: 'Begin with the heart'.*

3.4. A winding road – labyrinth

There are many ancient labyrinths in Ireland, like the Hollywood Stone in Wicklow, which was on the old pilgrim road to Glendalough. In recent times, a number of modern labyrinths have been constructed, among them, one at St Patrick's Purgatory in Lough Derg and another at the Rosminian House of Prayer in Glencomeragh.

The labyrinth was seen as symbolising a pilgrimage and came to be known as 'the sacred path'. Since a labyrinth can look like a maze, we need to be aware of the difference between them. A maze has dead ends and you can easily get lost. A labyrinth is a single sacred path that takes you right to the centre – you will not lose your way if you follow the path.

The labyrinth is a pattern with a purpose, as each step takes one closer to the centre. Once a person enters the labyrinth, it is like being drawn by a magnet towards the centre, always going the right direction, but wandering quite a lot along the way. While each step takes one closer to the centre, there is a sense of sometimes moving closer and sometimes moving away from it, but never leaving the circle. The labyrinth is a good image to convey our journey to God. It symbolises the spiritual life. Once we are within the circle of God's love, we remain there, unless we fall into the most awful lack of love and in desperation leave the circle.

Walking the labyrinth helps one to focus on what is happening in the inner life, in the heart and soul, where the quest and encounter takes place and God is revealed and experienced. It also helps one to get a sense of what happens in ordinary daily life, with its many twists and turns and all its changes. The labyrinth indicates that nothing is lost and no time or effort is wasted if you follow the path as it winds its way to the centre. The advice is to keep going, don't give up, and you will reach the centre. This holds true for our journey to God. The labyrinth symbolises the depth, richness and complexity of the journey to God by way of the heart and soul.

As John Moriarty discovered, and indeed many people discover, the journey to God is a winding road. The heart is the place of quest and encounter and is steeped in mystery much of the time. We are often groping in the dark as we try to find our way. The Christian sacraments, rituals, images and symbols help us. They provide us with 'a safe or at the very least a safer way of drawing nigh unto God' (John Moriarty). Pilgrimages also help people and have been very much part of the Christian tradition – with pilgrimages to Jerusalem, to Rome, to Compostela, to Canterbury and many other centres. When travel was difficult and dangerous and not possible for many people, there were local pilgrimages to honour the tradition of searching and being on a journey to encounter God. The labyrinth fits in here as a symbolic pilgrimage.

LABYRINTH

You may want to trace the path from the entrance to the centre – without crossing the line – and be mindful of your own journey to God, noting key turning points.

3.5. An 'oasis' on our journey

The oasis is a powerful image for people who live in desert lands. Perhaps we too can use it as an image to highlight important aspects of our journey by way of the heart into the mystery of God. Like the travellers in the desert, we have to stop at an oasis occasionally – a spiritual one.

In 1962, my sister travelled to Australia and I remember a letter that she wrote during that long journey by ship. She described various sights and there is one scene that has remained with me all these years. She got a view of the desert at some point and she described a camel caravan (camels and people) plodding through the lonely desert sands; she wondered where they had come from and where they were going – and were they likely to stop at an oasis along the way!

The scene came back to me a few years ago on a flight from London to Nairobi. We were crossing the southern Sahara desert as dawn broke. It was a breathtaking sight. From the window of the plane I could see the vast expanse of desert stretching to the horizon; there seemed to be no vegetation and no life that I could identify. But I thought that somewhere down there the camel caravans make their journeys through the desert and stop at an oasis to be refreshed and restored.

For the traveller in the desert there are few comforts – hour after hour of trudging through the desert sands in the burning heat takes its toll; it leaves one longing for water, shade and rest. The regular desert traveller knows where to find an oasis – that little green area in the desert where there is water surrounded by palm trees. At the oasis, life is preserved, nourished and sustained. It is a resting place for the weary traveller, who knows that life at the oasis has its own special traditions, which have to be respected by all who visit.[20]

At the oasis, everything is precious. Nobody would dare cut down a tree, or pollute the water or destroy what is around. The oasis has no favourites among those it receives; nobody can make any special claims because of race, culture, religion or status in life; all are equal and have the same rights and duties. People who stop at the oasis soon become friends. The travellers tell each other of the dangers along the way, the perils of the journey. They point to the safest routes and how to avoid the threat of robbers and wild animals. The oasis is the newsroom of the desert. The rest of the journey and indeed all hope of future journeys depends on how the visitors respect the oasis and look after one another when they are in need.

Like the travellers in the desert, we need an oasis where we can be restored and strengthened on our spiritual journey. At intervals, we need to come aside and rest awhile, so that we will be refreshed on our pilgrim way – with some silence, space and stillness in our day. Here, we are talking about the need for a time and place to rest and pray and share with one another, so that we can nurture our faith and trust in God who is calling us deeper into his divine life and love.

The oasis image highlights the importance of meeting and sharing with others on the journey. The travellers depend on this for their safety and security on the rest of the journey. Something similar happens on our spiritual journey. We too set out on a path into the desert, a path trodden by others, having faith that it will lead us where they said it would. We depend on all the help we can get as we travel along and feel our way into the mystery of God. We know that our journey is focused on Jesus and guided by his Holy Spirit, but we also know that those who have gone before us provide help and guidance in the quest for and encounter with God that takes place in our human hearts.

⬡

We are like travellers who, crossing the deserts of life, thirst for the living water, gushing and fresh, capable of quenching our deep desire for light, love, beauty and peace. We all feel this desire. And Jesus gives us this living water – the Holy Spirit who proceeds from the Father and whom Jesus pours into our hearts.
(Pope Francis)

3.6. Awareness of our need for God

A deep awareness of our need for God often goes hand in hand with an awakening to God's presence that takes place in our hearts. Take, for example, this story from the East:

> A disciple went to visit a spiritual master and told him he wanted to learn how to pray. 'Then here is how,' the Master replied, as he took hold of the disciple and plunged his head into a tub of water, and held it there while the disciple struggled to free himself. As he came out of the water gasping for breath, the disciple asked: 'Why did you do a thing like that?' The master calmly explained: 'In order to teach you that when you get to the point where you know you need God as much as you need air, then you will have learned to pray.'

It is a rather extreme way to teach a person about the need for God and the importance of prayer, but the point being made is clear. Prayer is present when we come to God in all our need. The encounter with God takes place 'in poverty and faith'. We are into prayer when we realise how much we yearn for and need God. The great Abraham Lincoln understood this and expressed it as such: 'I have been driven many times to my knees by the overwhelming conviction that I had absolutely no other place to go.'

Awareness of our need for God is sometimes born out of the depths of pain and suffering. When we feel such a need, we are into prayer, as we throw ourselves on the heart of God, crying out in anguish or perhaps in anger. In doing this, we realise that God's love is our hope and salvation, our refuge in times of trouble. Great suffering can bring one to a deeper awareness of the need for God – but this does not always happen; some people end up angry and bitter about the suffering they endure.

The yearning and need for God is also present when there is no obvious suffering or crisis in our lives. The longing for God can be felt as a restlessness that keeps us searching for love, for truth, for meaning and for purpose in life. This can lead us to realise that only God can fill our emptiness – that only God can satisfy our deepest heart's desire for love. Then we are on our way into the mystery – 'being drawn by the bonds of love, that only lovers will understand' (St Augustine).

Developing a prayerful attitude to life is central to our spiritual awakening – and awareness of our need for God. Such an attitude can be described as 'prayerfulness'. This is a word rich in meaning, like other similar words, such as thankfulness and mindfulness. Prayerfulness involves the heart; it involves 'heart-seeing' and 'heart-listening' and 'heart-living'. As the 'Little Prince' so wisely noted: 'It is only with the heart that we can see rightly; what is essential is invisible to the eye.'

Prayerfulness enables us to be aware of our need for God as we live our daily lives. It is fostered by the belief that God is not far from us, since it is 'in him we live and move and have our being' (Acts 17:28). Prayerfulness is the capacity to live life at a deeper level, finding silence in the midst of chaos and clarity in time of confusion. It is the gift of grace awakening our hearts to the need for God and God's abiding presence. Prayerfulness also helps us to be open to 'the gaze of Christ that purifies our hearts', and to the 'light of Christ that illumines the eyes of our hearts and teaches us to see everything in the light of his truth and his compassion for all people' (CCC 2715).

⊂※⊃

When I have learned to read God's Word in the book of my everyday life, then I am aware of a continuity and wholeness integrating all that I do in the course of the day. Everything promises to be an encounter with God – my sacred reading, my work and liturgical prayer, my interaction with others, my appreciation of nature, music and art. Everything becomes a way through which the Word of God speaks to me.
(St Bernard of Clairvaux)

3.7. The prayer of the heart

Contemplative prayer is 'the prayer of the heart' or 'the prayer of quiet' – as St Teresa of Avila described it. For her, contemplative prayer is 'nothing else than a close sharing between friends; it means taking time frequently to be alone with him who we know loves us'.

We know from experience that taking time frequently to be alone with a friend is important to human friendship and close sharing between friends involves the heart and feelings. Our friendship with God follows a similar pattern and is fostered by the 'prayer of the heart' – contemplative prayer.

Daniel O'Leary encourages us to develop a contemplative, prayerful habit of mind and heart that will greatly help us to see more clearly when we walk the streets of life:

> In so far as contemplative prayer is a temporary ceasing from our external activity, work and various ministries, this ceasing is only to equip us all the better to return to them with mind, heart and body renewed. We ponder in silence, in the sands of the spirit, only so as to be surer of the way we walk on the streets of life when we return. We enter into the solitude of the mountains from our travels in the busy valley, so as to see more clearly and with perspective, the hidden hazards and the potential wrong turnings of those travels. Jesus took his disciples aside to a quiet place, on occasion, so as to purify and intensify the spirit that animated their intense apostolate … If, then, we make this contemplative habit of mind and heart like second nature to us, the time we spend alone with God in personal prayer will be rich and transforming.[21]

Contemplative prayer is possible for everyone. It is always God's gift, available to anyone, at any time, in any place and at any age. But sometimes it is difficult to find time and space for it. Due to the endless demands of family life and work commitments, silence and stillness are often hard to find in daily living. All is not lost for people who find themselves in this situation. As we saw in Reflection 1.6, the great contemplative Carlo Carretto made the journey to God in the silence of the desert, while his mother made the same journey in her busy life at home, rearing a large family. Carlo felt she was as much a contemplative as he was, perhaps even more. The love of God flowed freely in her heart and life. She opened her heart and grew close to God through selfless giving. Her life and her prayer flowed into each other, with little time for silence. She welcomed God's presence in the endless opportunities for loving.

Another situation can arise, when we have plenty of quiet time alone, but we find it hard to pray. This can happen when we feel weighed down with cares and worries or we may be struggling to cope with serious illness. Pain and suffering can be very debilitating and can leave one with little energy or enthusiasm for prayer. We are advised not to burden ourselves with worry and guilt about not being able to pray at such times. We are encouraged to remember that God is always with us, helping us in our darkest hours – even if we do not feel it. In the crosses and complexities of life, God is present. If we can begin to sense this and glimpse the divine presence in the pain and anguish that are part of everyone's life at some stage, we are opening our hearts to God's abiding presence and into the prayer of the heart.

❧

Contemplative Prayer is a gaze of faith, fixed on Jesus. 'I look at him and he looks at me': this is what a certain peasant of Ars used to say to the holy Cure of Ars about his prayer before the tabernacle … Contemplative Prayer turns its gaze on the mysteries of the life of Christ. Thus it learns the 'interior knowledge of the Lord', the more to love him and serve him.
(CCC 2715)

We must keep our hearts open and wait for the heavenly dew to fall. Never forget to carry this thought with you in prayer.
(St Francis de Sales)

Chapter Four

'To See the Face of God'

'Come,' my heart says, 'seek his face'! Your face, Lord, do I seek.
Do not hide your face from me.
(Ps 27:8–9)

The face of God is that of a merciful father
who is always patient with us.
(Pope Francis)

4.1. 'I swear, I saw the face of God'

A newspaper photographer was in Ecuador in 1987 covering the earthquake that devastated many areas of the country. In the midst of the catastrophe, he witnessed something that touched him deeply. There was a line of people at a food distribution point. While the line was long, it was moving briskly. And in that line, at the very end, stood a young girl about twelve years of age. She waited patiently as those at the front of the line received a little rice, some canned food or fruit. Slowly but surely, she was getting closer to the front of that line, closer to the food. From time to time she would glance across the street. She did not notice the growing concern on the faces of those distributing the food.

The food was running out. Their anxiety began to show, but she did not notice. Her attention seemed always to focus on three children under the trees across the street.

At long last she stepped forward to get her food. But the only thing left was a lonely banana. The workers were almost ashamed but she did not seem to mind. Quietly she took the banana and ran across the street where the three small children waited – perhaps her two sisters and a brother. Very deliberately, she peeled the banana and carefully divided it into three equal parts. Placing the precious food into the eager hands of the three younger ones, she then sat down and licked the inside of the banana peel. Reflecting on this scene, the photographer said: 'In that moment, I swear, I saw the face of God.'

The photographer 'saw the face of God' in a simple act of kindness and love – in what the young girl did when she fed the younger children without a thought for herself.

'To see the face of God' is a very ancient and interesting phrase that occurs many times in the Bible. The psalmist prayed that he would see the face of God: '"Come," my heart says, "seek his face!" Your face, Lord, do I seek. Do not hide your face from me' (Ps 27:8–9). And: 'Let the light of your face shine on us, O Lord' (Ps 4).

We find the phrase used by Pope Benedict XVI, when he describes his book *Jesus of Nazareth* as his 'personal search for the face of the Lord'. In the introduction, he traces the origin of the phrase back to the Book of Exodus.

The photographer's story reminds us that the presence of God is all around us in the most ordinary experiences, especially where goodness and kindness are to be found; 'Where charity and love are found, God is present there.' We can 'see the face of God' in many precious moments of daily life. Such moments can be joyful and happy or they may be dark and lonely times. One can discover God in an act of kindness or in a hug from somebody. We can be aware of God in times of prayer and worship, or discover that God is present in an experience of hospitality, or in the support of family and friends that helps one to cope with the loss of a loved one.

God can be present in that 'something' that helps a person to keep going when things are difficult. When someone says 'I got strength from somewhere. I could not have coped without it,' there is a touch of God's presence here in the person's life. Spiritual writers tell us this is often the way it is; this is God's way of coming to us. For most people there are no great shining lights and visions, but just a gentle touch of God that awakens our hearts to his abiding presence in the ordinary events and experiences of life.

❧

May God let his face shine on you and be gracious to you.
May God uncover his face to you and bring you peace.
(Num: 6:24–6)

4.2. God is only a heartbeat away

We begin with a story from the East:

> 'How does a person seek God?' the disciple asked.
>
> 'The harder you seek,' the teacher said, 'the more distance you create.'
>
> 'So what can I do about that,' the student said.
>
> 'Just understand that the distance isn't there,' the teacher said.
>
> 'Does that mean that God and I are one,' the disciple said.
>
> 'Not one, not two,' the teacher said. 'But is that possible,' the disciple said.
>
> 'Not one, not two,' the teacher said, 'like the sun and its light, the ocean and its waves, the singer and the song, the dancer and the dance.'

This little story gives some deep insights that can help us in our quest for God. In our desire to find God, we need to go gently and avoid trying too hard to control things. At all times we try to remember that 'God is closer to us than we are to ourselves' (St Augustine). The images used in the story can help us to grasp this. Think of it like this: God is in us and in creation, as the sun is in its light, as the dancer is in the dance, as the voice of the singer is in a song and the ocean is in its waves. Here we have a helpful way to describe our closeness to God, who is 'hiding' in us and around us. In a special way, the human heart is the 'place of quest and encounter, in poverty and faith' – but even there, God hides:

> Even though God is within you, he is hidden. It is vital to know the place of his hiding, so that you can search for him with assuredness ... Since you know that in your heart, your beloved for whom you long, dwells hidden, your concern must be to be with him in hiding, and there in your heart you will embrace him.
> (*The Spiritual Canticle* of St John of the Cross)

We turn to St Paul for further insights into the interior and hidden nature of God's presence. He tells us that our hearts are God's temple (2 Cor 6:16), and that Christ lives in our hearts through faith (Eph 3:16). Reflecting on his own conversion, Paul wrote: 'God called me through his grace and chose to reveal his Son in me' (Gal 1:15–16). In another translation of that last phrase, we read: 'He chose to uncover his Son in me' – which implies that Christ was already present, but hidden!

In the rest of the passage following on from verse 16, we can see how Paul experienced and viewed his conversion. It was a personal encounter of the heart with Christ, who was revealed in him (not just to him, but in him), and this happened through a special revelation. He makes it clear that the experience itself is pure gift. We cannot control it, force it or make it happen. We can pray for it and hope for it. It is a grace that God can give to anybody, anywhere, anytime. It can have its dramatic moments, as it did for St Paul, but that may not be the way it is for you and me. St Ignatius of Loyola said 'grace is delicate, gentle, and delightful'. It can be compared to a drop of water penetrating a sponge. It does not clatter 'like a drop of water falling on a stone'. So we have to be open to the possibility of it happening this way for us – silently and gently. It is also possible to go for long periods without experiencing God's closeness but faith assures us that, experienced or not, God is still there – only a heartbeat away.

There is darkness at times and there are doubts on the journey of faith, but the sense of presence sustains us – even if we only manage 'to see the face of God' occasionally. We realise that we are not alone. Prayer, especially silent prayer, nourishes the sense of God's closeness. We are encouraged to take time frequently to be alone with God in silence: 'Let us make in ourselves a dwelling wholly at peace in which is always sung the canticle of love and gratitude, followed by silence, an echo of the very silence of God' (Elizabeth of the Trinity).

Why do we rush about to the top of heaven and the bottom of earth looking for God who is here at home with us, if only we would be at home with him.
(St Augustine)

4.3. Personal journeys

Paul Claudel, the great French writer and poet, had an experience that brought him to an awareness of God as a personal presence in his life. He came to recognise the face of God rather suddenly. It happened when he was eighteen. It was Christmas Day, and 'having nothing better to do', he attended vespers at Notre Dame Cathedral in Paris, hoping that the liturgy would provide him with inspiration for his poetry. Suddenly, he was overwhelmed by the awareness of God as a great personal reality, as 'somebody', and from that moment, his whole thought and life became dominated by the great presence so unexpectedly revealed to him which he summed up in this line: 'Lo! O God, You were Somebody all of a sudden.'

Leonard Cheshire, the founder of the Cheshire Homes, had a similar experience, though in very different circumstances. It happened when he and some friends were having a drink in a bar and the conversation turned to God – who or what God was. Cheshire, a professed agnostic, said that he thought God was just our own higher conscience, whereupon a girl in the party said firmly: 'That is utter rubbish. God is a person and you know that perfectly well.' With her words Cheshire got 'a flash of absolute certitude that here was the truth'. In that instant he recognised the face of God – a personal God. From that moment, God became for him the great ever-present reality who alone could give full meaning to his life and work.

Henri Nouwen travelled a different road as a believer all his life. Nevertheless, he struggled along the way and came to the conclusion in later life that he may have been trying too hard to find God and not allowing God to find him. He expressed it thus:

> For most of my life I have struggled to find God, to know God, to love God. I have tried hard to follow the guidelines of the spiritual life – pray always, work for others, read the scriptures. I have failed many times but always tried again, even when I was close to despair. Now I wonder whether I have sufficiently realised that during all this time God has been trying to find me, to know me, and to love me … God is looking into the distance, trying to find me, and longing to bring me home.[22]

Julian of Norwich was a great English mystic who travelled a very different way. In her book, *Showings of Divine Love*, she describes revelations that gave her deep insights into the mystery of God – the face of God. In the first revelation she was given a 'spiritual sight' in which she saw Christ holding a small globe in a loving embrace. She understood the globe to represent the world and all its peoples. She felt that God's infinite love was being revealed in the all-embracing love of Christ. In the final revelation, Christ assured her that even though we cannot understand suffering and sin now, in the end 'all will be well, all manner of thing will be well'. That assurance brought Julian comfort and strength as she travelled the road of hardship and suffering. She knew that, when the heart is weary and the soul is troubled, Christ is always reaching out to us and drawing us to himself, in a warm embrace.

All four people mentioned in this reflection had their own personal journeys to God and with God. They travelled different paths of spiritual awakening that enabled them 'to see the face of God'. The lives they lived led them deep into the mystery of the eternal and ever-present God who was always close to them, with them and in them, even though it took years for some of them to be aware of this and experience it.

These personal journeys remind us that each person finds his or her own way to God.

◈

The love of God is total, embracing all things; it is at once personal and transcendent. It beckons us to the path which leads to his heart of hearts.
(Paul Claudel)

4.4. Waiting to see the face of God

My time in Africa has made me appreciate the blessings of progress and prosperity at home. The nightmare of poverty and suffering continues for so many people in that continent. But I also feel that we can learn something from the pace of life, the spirituality and the wisdom of the people in the rural areas of Africa. They have a great sense of presence with each other and have a deep connection with the spiritual world. Their hearts and souls are engaged with the mystery of life and death. They have a capacity to be together and to wait and let a process take its course. There is no hurry in Africa, as the saying goes. This of course is not always true, especially for the cars and taxis on the roads! But there is some truth in the saying when you look more closely at their cultural practices.

When tragedy strikes people can hang around for days and weeks, doing very little, just being there with one another – waiting. They sit around the home of the family that has been struck by tragedy. They eat and drink and play music, especially the funeral drums, which can go on all night. Some people say that beating the drums is a way of keeping evil spirits at bay. There is little doubt that, with the insights they carry in their culture, they seem to realise that the wounds of loss and grief need lots of time for healing. They know there is no instant comfort. They also know that the face of God is hidden at such times and they have to wait for a while before they will see that face again. It will come, but it must be waited for. And they are good at doing just that.

For the people in the rural area of Kenya where I worked, God is there in the times of sorrow and waiting is the key. This comes from their culture but it is also the Christian way. We find a description of this approach in an article by Ronald Rolheiser. He offers suggestions about the best way to help people who are recently bereaved. He writes:

> What is needed more than our words is our presence, our sharing in the helplessness and our sharing in the waiting. In the first hours and days that follow a tragedy we don't need to speak a lot, we need to touch a lot. We simply need to be there.
>
> Moreover, the words that we do speak need to honour how deep and resistant to consolation the wound is. They should not

be an untimely balm – good medicine but bad timing. They must speak honestly to the senselessness of the situation and how disconsolate it leaves us … When we are in the middle of a storm we shouldn't pretend that the sun is shining or, indeed, that there is anything we can do to stop the storm. The task is to wait it out, together, hand in hand, offering each other the assurance that we aren't alone. Waiting it out is precisely what is required … Consolation will come eventually, but is must be waited for …[23]

So in the Christian and the African cultural way, being together, supporting each other and patiently waiting are regarded as essential to help people cope with tragic loss, grief and pain. When there is great sadness, it can take days, weeks, months or even years to come to healing and back into the light – to see the face of God once more. It can be a long, dark road to recovery from a tragedy when a loved one dies of illness, or is killed in a senseless accident, or worse still when someone commits suicide. Our God does not always save us from such tragedies, but we believe in God's infinite mercy and that his consolation will come, that soon again we will see His face, which we 'have loved long since, but lost a while'.

෧෯

Wait for the Lord; be strong, let your heart take courage;
wait for the Lord.
(Ps 27)

4.5. Jesus is the human face of God

I remember the first time Midnight Mass on Christmas Night was celebrated in our local church. It was something special. Young and old set out for the church. There were few motorcars in those days. Some people walked or cycled, while others travelled by horse cart, or by donkey cart. There was a wonderful atmosphere, with the darkness of the night, the stream of lights heading for the church and the lighted candles in the windows of all the houses. The church too seemed different. The dim light gave the place a mysterious air. The congregation was somewhat more alive than usual, with a few individuals showing a lot of devotion (or lack of it!), because the hours before Mass had been spent in one of the village pubs. Most of all, for us children, it was the crib that grabbed our attention – the strange little cave-like structure with the unusual figures brought the events of that first Christmas night to life. It took us back to the holy family in the stable at Bethlehem – a mother, Mary, and father, Joseph, and the infant Jesus in the manger.

I expect that a mother or father can relate to the first Christmas night with special insight. The birth of a child is a great occasion for parents. All mothers and fathers know their newborn child is special, and this would be true for Mary and Joseph. The child Jesus was very special indeed – in him the 'Word is made flesh and lives among us.' Jesus is 'Emmanuel – a name which means God is with us'. In Jesus we meet God face-to-face. This is the mystery of the Incarnation. The scene represented in the crib is the way God chose to enter our world and become one of us human beings.

Jesus was born in a stable – stark and poor. Coming from a farming family, I remember how warm and cosy the house for the cows felt at night. But still, it is hard to imagine a child being born in such a place, and even more remarkable a child who is the Son of God, who is revealing the face of God to us. For sure, God's ways are not our ways. There is no doubt that the way God chose to reveal himself on that first Christmas Night took many people by surprise; they did not expect the Messiah to come in this way. Only the shepherds and the Wise Men were able to recognise that the baby in the manger was God-with-us.

Jesus could have been born to a rich family, but people would say it was because they had money. He could have been born to a powerful family and people would say it was because they were high and mighty. He could have been born to a famous family and people would say it was because they had the world at their feet. But there has to be more to the way God came than what people would say. God chose to be born to very ordinary parents (in the world's eyes), in the humblest and poorest of circumstances. He came into our world as a helpless child, powerless, weak and vulnerable. Love is his way; humility is his way; simplicity is his way. Before Jesus ever preached a word, the message was there from the moment of his birth in his own flesh and blood – a child in a manger in the stable at Bethlehem revealing the face of God in love, humility, simplicity and poverty. Jesus is the human face of God.

❧

He is the image of the invisible God, the firstborn of all creation, for in him all things were created, in heaven and on earth, visible and invisible. For in him all the fullness of God was pleased to dwell, and through him to reconcile all things to himself, whether on earth or in heaven, making peace by the blood of his cross.
(Col 1:12)

And is it true,
This most tremendous tale of all,
Seen in a stained-glass window's hue,
A baby in an ox's stall?
The maker of the stars and sea
Become a child on earth for me?
(John Betjeman, 'Christmas')

4.6. The Spirit reveals the face of God

I wrote the following on a beautiful Pentecost Sunday morning when I was in Kenya:

> As I step out into the morning here in Luanda, near the equator, I am very aware of the light and life that is so much part of our experience almost every morning in the tropics. The rising sun casts a soft warm glow across the countryside and the birds are singing to their hearts' content. I get a sense that the whole of creation is being renewed with life and light. The circle of life continues with humans, birds and animals; change and growth are taking place night and day, while I sleep, while I am awake – how, I do not know.
>
> The cycle of life, death and new life is present before my eyes in the world of nature. The seed falls on the ground and dies and produces a rich harvest. The divine energy is flowing freely all around me. I can steep myself in it and soak myself in it. I can let it seep into my heart and soul and feel the touch of God's Spirit deep within my being. I can feel God's embrace – see God's face. I can sense the reality of the Spirit's power and presence. This is what we celebrate at Pentecost: the outpouring of God's Spirit into the hearts of the disciples and into our hearts and the whole of creation.

That Pentecost morning was a new awakening for me – at least in a small way. I became more aware that the light and life of the Spirit flows through all creation and transforms it together with our human hearts and lives. The Spirit pours out his gifts, revealing the face of God and drawing us into the mystery of God. We are being transfigured into God's likeness; such is the influence of the Spirit (2 Cor 3:18). In the Letter to the Romans, we are told that: 'All who are led by the Spirit of God, are children of God ... When we cry "Abba! Father!", it is that very Spirit bearing witness' (Rom 8:14–16).

In the words of *Redemptoris Missio*: 'The love of God, the Spirit of God is present in people's hearts, in their history, in their culture, and in their religion. The Holy Spirit, with His gifts, is there waiting for the person to awaken to the reality.'

Scripture can help us to awaken to the reality of the God and nourish the work of the Spirit within us. It can help us to open our hearts to God's presence and love in a way that leads to a deep spiritual awakening and change of heart.

St Augustine described how it happened for him.[24] When he was in the garden of his lodgings, feeling very confused and distressed, he heard what he thought was the voice of a child saying: 'Take and read – take up and read.' At first, he wondered if this was a chant that children used in some kind of game but he could not recall hearing it anywhere.

He then picked up the Bible and read from the Letter to the Romans: 'Not in reveling and drunkenness, not in debauchery and licensiousness, not in quarreling and jealousy. Instead, put on the Lord Jesus Christ, and make no provision for the flesh, to gratify its desires' (Rom 13:13–14). This was the moment of his conversion: 'No further wished I to read, nor was there need to do so. Instantly, in truth, at the end of this sentence, it was as if before a peaceful light streaming into my heart, all the dark shadows of doubt fled away.'

In this way, the Spirit revealed the presence of God, the face of God, in Augustine's heart and his life was changed forever.

⌘

The presence, warmth and light of Christ's Spirit should remain with us (within us), and shine forth in our entire lives. Communion with Christ helps us to 'see' the signs of the Divine presence in the world, and to 'manifest' it to all whom we encounter.
(The Year of the Eucharist, 26)

4.7. Compassion reveals the face of God

There are times when the face of God is hidden. This can be for
short periods or it can last for weeks, months or even years.
Sometimes when the clouds come down and darkness falls
around us we can no longer experience the presence of God or
see the face of God. We feel that God is distant or absent. This is
likely to happen when there is serious suffering, loss, grief and
pain that leave our hearts weary and our souls greatly burdened.
The darkness that comes with suffering is never far away. In the
words of Kahlil Gibran: 'Joy and sorrow go hand in hand like
brother and sister, when one sits down at your table the other is
asleep on your bed.' We can say the same about light and
darkness; they go hand in hand in life for most people.

In her book *Sharing the Darkness*, Dr Sheila Cassidy uses
'darkness' as an image for human suffering. She herself suffered
for her solidarity with the poor and oppressed in Chile. When she
returned to England, she spent a number of years working with
the terminally ill in a hospice. In working as a doctor with the
poor and the sick she was sharing in the darkness. This is where
compassion led her and leads many committed Christians in our
world. Compassion means 'to suffer with' or 'to journey with
others through their suffering' – sharing their darkness.
Compassion can often reveal the face of God to people in times
of suffering; they find that somebody cares and is there to help
them – as Liam Lawton wrote in his song 'The Cloud's Veil':
'Even when the dark clouds veil the sky, you are by my side.'

There is also another kind of darkness when the face of God
is hidden even though there is no serious suffering – as described
above. This is 'the dark night of faith' when a person goes for
short or long periods without an experience of the presence of
God. A priest who read my earlier book *Going the Heart's Way*
described it thus:

> I can honestly say that I thoroughly enjoyed the book ... but I felt
> some envy in the sections about the personal experience of God
> in one's life as that is something that I have always ached for and
> my favourite psalm passage is: 'My soul longs for the Lord like a
> dry, dreary land without water.' I have been told over and over
> again by spiritual directors that I have to accept my prosaic (and

at times atheistic!) temperament and not to get too worked up about not having that experience. However, one can always hope! Instead, better to concentrate on love and service, also central themes in your book, as something equally acceptable to God.

When the memoirs of Blessed Mother Teresa were published after her death, people were surprised to find that for many years she struggled to feel God's presence in her life. In a sense, the face of God was hidden from her at an experiential level. We cannot help wondering how this could happen to a person who showed so much love and compassion as she lived her life caring for the poor and needy. She was a woman of extraordinary faith and trust in God and yet she went through many years not feeling God's presence. To find that Mother Teresa travelled this road brings comfort to those who do not feel God's presence in a definite way on the journey of faith. Indeed, there are few of us who do not feel God is far away or absent at some stage, but the glimpses of God's face that we get from time to time enable us to keep going.

We may recall the little phrase from Carl Jung that was quoted in the introduction: 'Invoked or not invoked, God is present' – and we can rephrase it: 'Felt or not felt, God is still there.' Our faith assures us that we live in God's abiding presence all the time even when we do not experience that presence. We are encouraged to keep going when the face of God is hidden, not to give up but to persevere on our journey into the mystery of God.

St John of the Cross describes 'the dark night of faith' in his beautiful poems: 'The Living Flame of Love' and 'On a Dark Night …'. These poems are based on his own experience of his journey into the mystery of God. They focus on 'the dark night' but also on the 'living flame of love' burning in his heart, as he made the journey in stillness through the darkness. For him, the 'dark night' was attractive and positive despite the obvious suffering and distress it caused him; it was a case of, 'oh night more loving than the dawn'.

⁂

Even though the rain hides the stars, even though the mist swirls the hills, even when the dark clouds veil the sky, you are by my side. Even when

the sun shall fall in sleep, even when at dawn the sky shall weep, even in the night when storms shall rise, you are by my side.
(Liam Lawton: The Cloud's Veil)

CHAPTER FIVE

Divine Love Opens Wide Its Arms

*Neither painting nor sculpting can any longer
quieten my soul, turned now to that Divine Love,
which on the cross, to embrace us, opened wide its arms.*
(Michelangelo)

5.1. Divine love opens wide its arms

In the life we live, awakening to God's abiding presence, we look towards Jesus: 'Keep your gaze fixed upon Jesus' (Pope Francis). In many of the reflections we try to do this. We do it especially in this present chapter with the reflections focused on his Passion, death and Resurrection, and his presence with us in the Eucharist.

As a student in Rome many years ago, I got a chance to visit the Sistine Chapel a number of times. The main attraction for visitors is Michelangelo's famous painting on the ceiling of the chapel; the painting took four years to complete – 1508–1512. It is really a series of paintings, telling of God's creation of Adam and Eve and ending with the story of salvation – through the prophets and the ancestors of Christ. The painting is truly magnificent. Each time I saw the painting, I was moved by the experience. In addition to the Sistine Chapel, St Peter's Basilica is always on the list of places to visit. It is home to Michelangelo's famous sculpture the *Pieta*. The *Pieta* is a depiction of the body of Jesus on the lap of his mother Mary when he was taken down from the cross. For centuries, this sculpture has touched the hearts of visitors. It tells a story of tender motherly love and personal grief.

Michelangelo was also the architect of the plans for St Peter's Basilica. He is regarded as one of the most famous artists in history – as a painter, a sculptor and an architect. He died in 1564 at the age of eighty-nine. His final years were marked with times when he was very troubled and sometimes worried about the salvation of his own soul. Towards the end of his life, he lost interest in painting and sculpture and turned to Christ's suffering and death on the cross. This brought him some comfort and relief. On the experience, he wrote:

> My life's journey has finally arrived, after a stormy sea, in a fragile boat, at the common port, through which all must pass to render an account and explanation of their every act, evil and devout ... Neither painting nor sculpting can any longer quieten my soul, turned now to that divine love, which on the cross, to embrace us, opened wide its arms.[25]

Pope Benedict XVI points us in the same direction, assuring us that by contemplating Christ's death on the cross we come to realise that God is love:

The divine activity of God that takes on dramatic form when, in Jesus Christ, it is God himself who goes in search of the stray sheep, a suffering and lost humanity. When Jesus speaks in his parables of the shepherd who goes after the lost sheep, of the woman who looks for the lost coin, of the father who goes to meet and embrace his prodigal son, these are no mere words; they constitute an explanation of his very being and activity. This is love in its most radical form. Christ's death on the cross is the culmination of this love; by contemplating the Crucifixion we can understand that God is love. (*God is Love*, p. 12.)

In the Dominican Abbey in Kilkenny, there is a curious little statue called *The Throne of Grace*; it dates from around 1400. It expresses rather well what Michelangelo and Pope Benedict put into words, namely, that in the Crucifixion of Christ, divine love opened wide its arms to embrace us. The statue depicts God the Father sitting on a throne, holding the cross bearing His dying son between his knees. The Holy Spirit is depicted in the form of a dove, sitting on top of the cross, symbolising the Love that unites the Father and Son. Jesus, with arms outstretched, is hanging on the cross that the Father is holding close to his heart, which is the source of the 'divine love which, on the cross to embrace us, opened wide its arms'.

❧

Keep your gaze fixed upon Jesus; in him all the anguish and all the longing of the human heart finds fulfilment.
(Pope Francis)

What sinner can be so hardened as not to go instantly and cast himself at the feet of the Saviour when he knows the tender love with which Jesus Christ is prepared to embrace him and carry him on his shoulders.
(St Alphonsus Ligouri)

5.2. Jesus on the cross

In his Christmas meditation one year, the late Cardinal Hume told about a Londoner, who was on his way home from work one evening before Christmas and felt drawn to Westminster Cathedral. He could not explain why, as he had long ago abandoned his faith. He may have drifted to the church because he was feeling troubled. Having entered the building he came across the Christmas crib. There were men, women and children all around, praying. He glanced at several of the faces of those at prayer. They seemed to be in possession of a precious secret. They looked at ease with themselves. He envied them. Then, turning away from the crib, his eyes settled on the large crucifix hanging from the dome of the cathedral. He was quite taken aback at the sight of it – a man hanging on a cross, tortured, abandoned, dead.

The visitor sat and gazed at the crucifix. Slowly, it gave up its secret as he began to see in the figure on the cross the faces of people suffering in the world: people slaughtered in Rwanda, people starving in Sudan – flies crawling all over their parched skin, eyes staring, no longer appealing for help, but waiting, just waiting, for the end. He could see the grieving parents of loved ones killed in an accident, and the suffering of the mentally and physically sick. All human suffering seemed to be gathered up and made his own by the man on the cross. Then he heard singing. It came from far away, from behind the main altar. It was quite beautiful. As he listened, his spirit seemed to be carried upwards into another sphere. He soon realised that he was praying and became aware that Jesus on the cross was revealing the love of God for all people. He was deeply moved.

When the visitor was leaving, an old man at the back of the cathedral wished him a 'Happy Christmas'. For the first time in his life, the visitor understood what it meant. He felt some peace and calm had entered his troubled soul as he left the cathedral a much happier man than when he arrived. Later, he would come to understand that the crib, the cross and the altar (the Eucharist) belong together; the child in the manger is the same person as the man on the cross and the Risen Lord present in the Eucharist.

The man's visit to the cathedral turned into an occasion of grace for him. He was given a glimpse of the depths of the mystery of the Passion and death of Jesus. Soon his heart opened to the deep secrets about the man on the cross. He realised that it is all about love. He was aware that human suffering seemed to be gathered up and made his own (redeemed) by Jesus as he opened wide his arms on the cross. He saw the same Jesus suffering today in each person who suffers and is in need. He realised that Jesus identifies with every human person and that he has a special care for the lost, the lonely, those who suffer, those who are hungry, thirsty, strangers, sick, those who are in prison – all who suffer (Mt 25:31–46).

Jesus identifies with us in such a way that he is intensely personal in our lives: 'It is no longer I who live, but it is Christ who lives in me' (Gal 2:20). We are 'one' with Christ – this is what he prayed for, 'that they may all be one; as you Father are in me, and I am in you, may they also be one in us' (Jn 17:21). This being 'one' is brought about by the divine love that flows from the heart of the Father, through the Son on the cross, in the Holy Spirit: 'as the Father makes himself visible in the Son, so the Son makes himself present in the Holy Spirit'. And the Holy Spirit is present in the world today when we respond to the love that is poured into our hearts by that same Spirit and begin to live it and share it with others. We are now the hands and heart of Jesus reaching out to those who suffer.

⊰⊱

On the cross, Jesus is united with every person who suffers from hunger in the world; He is united with the parents who suffer as they see their children become victims of drugs. He is united with those who suffer for their beliefs, or simply for the colour of their skin. On the cross, Jesus is united with many young people who have lost faith in political institutions, or in the Church, or even in God, because of the counter-witness of Christians.
(Pope Francis)

5.3. The 'Seven Last Words' of Jesus

There are various ways in which we can contemplate the Passion and Crucifixion of Jesus. Whatever way we choose, we are contemplating how much God loves us, and how divine love, on the cross, opened wide its arms to embrace us: 'God loved the world so much that he gave his only Son, so that everyone who believes in him may not perish but may have eternal life' (Jn 3:16).

We can journey with Jesus in his final days and hours of suffering by doing the 'Stations of the Cross' or by reading passages from the Gospel accounts of his Passion and Crucifixion. The Stations of the Cross is a devotion that helps many Christians to spend time reflecting on the Passion and death of Jesus. I remember as a young boy going to the church on Good Friday with my parents to do the Stations and I can still feel the atmosphere that was in the church as people quietly went from Station to Station. There was a sense of awe and mystery in the church on that special day. This was long before we had Holy Week Ceremonies in our local church – we had not even heard of them!

There is also another way that has a long tradition in the Church. It focuses on the seven 'Lasts Words' (phrases) of Jesus on the cross. The last words spoken by a person on the point of death have great significance. We tend to remember them and cherish them and ponder them long after the person has died. So it is not surprising that the 'Last Words' of Jesus on the cross have great significance for us. Reflection on these words can lead us into the depths of the mystery of the Lord's Passion and Crucifixion. There is a special devotion around the seven 'Last Words' that can be traced back to the twelfth century. St Bonaventure and other authors, mainly Franciscans, brought together the seven 'Last Words' that Jesus spoke on the cross – as they are recorded in the Gospels.

The seven 'Last Words' are as follows:

1. 'Father, forgive them, for they do not know what they are doing.' (Lk 23:34)
2. 'Today you will be with me in Paradise.' (Lk 23:43)
3. 'Woman, Behold your Son … Behold your mother.' (Jn 19:26–27)

4. 'My God, my God, why have you forsaken me?' (Mk 15:34)
5. 'I thirst.' (Jn 19:28)
6. 'It is finished.' (Jn 19:30)
7. 'Father, into your hands I commend my spirit.' (Lk 23:46)

The seven 'Last Words' (phrases) have a certain structure to them. The first is addressed to the Father, as is the last and the one in the centre (the cry of anguish). Everything happens in the context of Jesus' relationship with the Father. He does the Father's will and reveals the Father's love, bringing us all into the circle of that love in the shelter of the Trinity. Jesus is 'the divine love, which on the cross, opens wide its arms to embrace us'.

❦

Prayer focused on the seven 'Last Words'
Perhaps you can stay with one of the phrases for a while and ponder it deep in your heart. Or you may want to use the following prayer that focuses on the 'Last Words':

> O my Lord Jesus Christ, who was born for me in a stable, lived for me a life of pain and sorrow, and died for me upon a cross, say for me in the hour of my death: 'Father forgive', and to your Mother: 'behold your child'. Say to me yourself: 'this day you shall be with me in paradise'. O my Saviour, leave me not and forsake me not.
>
> 'I thirst' for you and long for your fountain of living water – my days pass quickly along, soon all will be consummated for me – 'into your hands I commend my spirit' – now and for ever. Amen. (St Elizabeth Ann Seton – first American-born canonised saint)

5.4. 'Jesus – I want this Jesus'

When Cardinal Timothy Dolan was a priest in Washington, D.C., he conducted the Good Friday liturgy in a hospice for AIDS patients, which was run by the Missionaries of Charity. When the ceremony was over two sisters led him upstairs so that the bedridden patients could kiss the feet of our Lord on the cross.[26]

As he went from bed to bed, he noticed an emaciated man in the corner who seemed agitated. When he began to approach the man's bed, the sister warned him that this man was unusually violent, and had actually attempted to bite the attending sisters a number of times. Slowly and cautiously, Fr Dolan approached and carefully extended the crucifix, which the man grasped and kissed – not the feet, but the face of the crucified Jesus. He then lay back down, exhausted.

The next day, Holy Saturday, the man asked to see Fr Dolan and when Fr Dolan was approaching him, he whispered, 'I want to be baptised!' and went on to explain why he desired baptism:

> I know nothing of Christianity or the Catholic Church. In fact, I have hated religion all my life. All I do know is that from the three months I have been here dying, these sisters are always happy! When I curse them, they look at me with compassion in their eyes. Even when they clean up my vomit, bathe my sores, and spoon-feed me, there is radiance in their eyes. All I know is that they have joy and I don't. When I ask them in desperation why they are so happy, all they answer is 'Jesus'. I want this Jesus. Baptise me and give me this Jesus! Give me joy!

He was baptised and he died at 3.15 the next morning – Easter Sunday.

The slow death of an AIDS patient is very distressing. During my time in Africa I have seen dying AIDS patients and they travel a very long, painful, lonely road. The stigma of AIDS and the suffering that the disease brings leads them to literally waste away physically and emotionally. The patient is often thrown there in the corner of a small hut, lying on a blanket, looking sickly and emaciated. They often do not have the care and company that a person dying of another disease would have. We can assume that the patient in the story had travelled a similar lonely road. His human heart was covered with a crust of anger and bitterness and his nature was violent. Yet the sight of the crucifix stirred something in that same human heart. There was a spark of the divine that had not been extinguished and it was being touched and awakened. Something stirred, moved, changed deep within him.

From what the man said, we can assume that he recognised Jesus on the cross as the same Jesus that the sisters spoke about. The goodness and love that he experienced was not lost on him. They were doing what they were doing, caring for him and loving him, in the name of Jesus. This is the Jesus who does not break the crushed reed nor quench the wavering flame. The man came to know this when they washed him and cleaned him with joy and radiance in their eyes, in spite of his violent and angry attitude and actions.

The crucifix symbolises divine love opening wide its arms to embrace everyone. It was this love that touched the sisters' hearts and was expressed in their daily ministry. The living, loving actions of the sisters were the fruit of their own experience and knowledge of the crucified Lord, who suffered and died for all. The crucified Christ was no stranger to the sisters, whether it was Jesus on the cross or Jesus in the dying AIDS patient in front of them. The sisters knew in their hearts that Jesus on the cross reveals divine love opening wide its arms. They also knew that 'in the least of our brothers and sisters, we find Jesus, and in Jesus, we find God' (Pope Benedict). In Jesus we find God's abiding love and presence, and Jesus is present in people and places that can surprise us all.

⬲

Faith tells us that God has given his Son for our sakes and gives us the victorious certainty that it is really true ... It thus transforms our impatience and our doubts into the sure hope that God holds the world in his hands.
(Pope Benedict, *God is Love*, p. 39)

5.5. Gaze on the crucified Christ

In the ways of praying that St Dominic proposed and practised, one's gaze is fixed on the crucified Christ and the love that is revealed in his Passion and Crucifixion.

St Dominic sometimes prayed standing – with his head bowed to express humility. At other times he prayed lying prostate on the ground to ask forgiveness for his sins. We are told that he often prayed kneeling in penance before the crucifix, with his arms outstretched, opening his mind and heart to the infinite love revealed in Christ crucified.

After celebrating Mass, he would sit quietly in meditation for a long period gazing at the crucifix. He set no time limit to his meditation. This kind of prayer he regarded as having a more intimate, fervent and soothing dimension to it. During those periods of prayer, he experienced closeness to God so intensely that others saw his reactions of joy or tears, and sometimes his face would light up. Afterwards he would humbly resume his daily work.

When St Dominic was travelling, passing through valleys and across the hills, he would contemplate the beauty of creation. Prayers of praise and thanksgiving would well up in his heart as he was aware of God's many gifts all around him, and especially for the greatest wonder of all: the redemptive work of Christ – that God our Father and creator sent his only Son to be our Saviour, to suffer and die for us. Dominic was inwardly in touch with the crucified Christ, while appreciating and enjoying God's gifts in creation. He stressed that only a relationship with God and with Christ crucified gives one the strength and courage to live through all the events of life, especially times of suffering and anguish.

St Dominic encouraged people to gaze on Christ crucified and have a relationship with Christ in his suffering. This is the source of faith, true knowledge, and love of others – the three main criteria for Christian discernment on our journey to union with God. Gazing on Christ crucified opens the door of the heart to an experience of Christ's infinite love for us: 'no one has greater love than this, to lay down one's life for his friends; you are my friends' (Jn 15:13–14). This is the love that flowed from the heart of Jesus on the cross and led him to promise the man on the cross beside him that 'today you will be with me in Paradise' (Luke

23:43). He spoke these words to a man who was a thief, by his own admission. The love of Christ opened wide its arms to embrace that man and indeed all people in every age – with the promise of redemption, salvation, deliverance, and forgiveness.

Contemplating Christ's Passion and Crucifixion helps us to feel our way into this great mystery at the heart of our faith. It helps us to feel for Christ as we journey with him in his suffering during his last days and hours on earth. We 'remember' the road he travelled and we enter into what he experienced – in our own limited way. This will help us to experience Christ's love. Calvary is full of suffering and rejection but it is shot through with love and compassion. The more we focus on the Crucifixion, the deeper will our awareness be of the radical nature of Christ's love for us. St Paul wrote:

> Jesus, who, though he was in the form of God, did not regard equality with God as something to be exploited, but emptied himself, taking the form of a slave, being born in human likeness. And being found in human form, he humbled himself and became obedient to the point of death – even death on a cross (Phil 2:5–11).

In *The Spiritual Exercises*, St Ignatius suggests that when gazing at Christ on the cross, we should try to have a conversation with him:

> Imagine Christ our Lord present before you upon the cross and begin to speak with him and listen to what He has to say to you. Then reflect on your own response to Christ's love – As you behold Christ in this plight, nailed to the cross, ponder upon what presents itself to your mind and heart.

❧

We adore you, O Christ, and we praise you, because by your holy cross you have redeemed the world.

Father, everything Jesus did and everything he said while on earth, even the insults, the spitting, the buffeting, the cross and the grave, all that was nothing but yourself speaking in the Son, appealing to us by your divine love, and stirring up our love for you.
(William Saint-Thierry)

5.6. To 'see the risen Lord'

The crucified Christ is now the Risen Lord – revealing the divine love that on the cross opened wide its arms to embrace us. This takes us on a journey from the Crucifixion to the resurrection, from darkness to light, from death to new life. It is a journey to faith in the Risen Christ – a journey that can take time, as we see from what happened with Mary Magdalene and the disciples.

According to St John's Gospel (Jn 20:11–18), Mary Magdalene was the first to 'see the Risen Lord' – though it took her a while to recognise him. As we read about what happened, we have to remember the attitude to women in Jewish society at that time. They were oppressed and discriminated against. They were in the same category as children and shepherds and were not far removed from the level of slaves. They would not be seen as reliable witnesses. So this makes what happened all the more remarkable; Mary Magdalene was the first to encounter the Risen Christ. She was the first to go to the tomb; she went while it was still dark. She came running to Peter to tell him what she found: 'They have taken away my Lord, she said, and I do not know where they have laid him.' Then Peter and John rushed to the tomb. After they had gone into the empty tomb and seen the linen cloths, they returned home. They did not 'see the Risen Lord'.

And now comes a very interesting part, as Mary stayed there outside the tomb, weeping. She stooped down to look inside and saw two angels, who asked her why she was weeping. Suddenly, she turned round and Jesus was standing there, but she did not recognise him. She thought he was the gardener. It was only when He called her name that she recognised him. Then Jesus said to her: 'Do not hold on to me ... But go to the brothers and say to them "I am ascending to my Father and your Father, to my God and your God"' (Jn 20:17). So Mary went and told the disciples that she had 'seen the Lord' and that he had said these things to her.

While Mary had some difficulty recognising Jesus the Risen Lord, the disciples found it even more difficult. It was a very gradual journey into the light of faith. They were full of fear and doubts and hesitation: 'they were in a state of alarm and fright, as they thought they were seeing a ghost'. They stood there dumbfounded and Jesus asked them: 'Why are you so agitated and why are these doubts rising in your hearts?' So we learn that faith in the Risen Lord did not come quickly or easily for them.

So too for the two disciples on the road to Emmaus – they were downcast (Lk 24:13–35); they had lost hope and were going off into the countryside, away from the community. They were disappointed – lost in the darkness of their own hearts. But Jesus was there to help them and reveal to them the real meaning of his Passion and death, and their hearts burned within them. They finally recognised Him in the 'breaking of the bread' – in the Eucharist.

We need not be too surprised if we too have doubts and difficulties on the journey of faith; we can find ourselves groping in the dark, with fear and hesitation. Like Mary Magdalene and the disciples, we can feel upset when we cannot 'see the Risen Lord' in our prayer, in our worship or in the experiences of daily life. But, like Mary and the disciples, we may come upon him unexpectedly and discover that he has been with us all the time, ready to bring us hope and healing, strength and courage, light and life.

❧

Only in Christ crucified and risen can we find salvation and redemption. With him, evil, suffering and death do not have the last word, because he gives us hope and life. He has transformed the cross from being an instrument of hate, defeat and death, to being a sign of love, victory, triumph and life.
(Pope Francis)

5.7. 'In a crumb of bread'

The Risen Lord is now present among us. This takes us from Christ on the Cross to Christ with us in the Eucharist. Whenever and wherever it is celebrated 'in a crumb of bread' the whole mystery is present.

I go back to an experience that I shall always remember. I celebrated Mass on Christmas Day with a small community in a remote village of Luanda parish, western Kenya. The church was a simple structure with mud walls and a thatched roof – not in very good condition. This was a 'Mass centre' in the humblest of circumstances. Many people and lots of children crowded into the little church. The place was packed and felt very hot, with plenty of warm air coming through the holes in the walls where the mud had fallen away or been washed away by the rain. The congregation sang and clapped and danced in the small space available. There was much life and energy, and a great sense of reverence.

I was more aware than usual of the great mystery that we were celebrating – the Risen Christ present with us in the Eucharist – revealing the divine love flowing from the heart of God that reaches out to embrace everyone. It is the same wherever it is celebrated. It can be in a big cathedral or church in a city or town, or it can be in the simplest village church in Africa. It can be in Croke Park, as it was for the closing of the Eucharistic Congress in Dublin. It is the same Eucharist wherever people gather and the Risen Christ is present. I remember the 'Station (House) Masses' at home in Kerry as something very special for all present. I recall stories about the 'Mass Rocks'[27] when Christ was present among his people in the most ordinary and extraordinary situations – when people were often struggling and in danger. I think of the poem 'The Great Hunger', in which the poet Patrick Kavanagh presents a number of individuals struggling through life with great difficulty, yet enjoying moments of experience that opened their hearts to the mystery of Christ's presence. The bachelor farmer character, Paddy Maguire, expressed this in prayer: 'O Christ, that is what you have done for us: In a crumb of bread the whole mystery is.'

Pope Benedict expressed the same belief this way:

To adore the body of Christ means to believe that there, in that piece of bread, there really is Christ who gives meaning to our lives, to the immense universe as well as to the smallest creature, and to all of human history as well as the briefest existence. (Pope Benedict XVI)

In every Eucharist, in that 'crumb of bread', Christ is truly present and so is the whole mystery of his Incarnation, Passion, Crucifixion, Resurrection, Ascension and Pentecost. We can say that in the Eucharist we truly encounter that divine love that on the cross opened wide its arms to embrace us. This is our Eucharist, so glorious and mysterious, where we can welcome and receive Christ into our hearts and lives and homes in the most personal and intimate way.

Let us hope that we will never lose our sense of wonder, our sense of awe and gratitude, when we celebrate the Eucharist. We know that every time we do this, divine love opens wide its arms to embrace us, and in doing so, renews our commitment to give expression to that divine love every day, in the lives we live:

> The Eucharist should lead us to exclaim, as did the apostles after encountering him risen: 'We have seen the Lord' ... The presence, warmth and light of Christ should remain with us and shine forth in our entire lives. Communion with Christ helps us to 'see' the signs of God's [abiding] presence in the world and to 'manifest' it to all whom we encounter (The Year of the Eucharist, p. 26).

~~~

The truth of our union with Jesus Christ in the Eucharist is tested by whether or not we love our fellow men and women; it is tested by how we treat others, especially our families; husbands and wives, children and parents, brothers and sisters. It is tested by whether or not we try to be reconciled to our enemies, or whether or not we forgive those who hurt and offend us. It is tested by whether we practice in life what our faith teaches us.
(Pope John Paul II, Ireland, 1979)

CHAPTER SIX

With Love beyond All Telling

No one has greater love than this,
to lay down one's life for one's friends.
(Jn 15:13)

6.1. The heart of Jesus goes out to all

I was driving to the airport in Nairobi, Kenya, one evening. The traffic was dreadful, barely moving and often stopped in one spot for long periods. There was a bus in front of me. On the back window of the bus, there was a big picture of the Sacred Heart of Jesus. It was a most unlikely sight in the midst of the madness and mayhem that is Nairobi traffic. The public service vehicles in Kenya often display posters and pictures, but usually they feature Arsenal and Manchester United! So I was quite surprised to see the Sacred Heart looking down at me. As I gazed at the face with the gentle, loving features and the long hair, I felt a little calmer and less frustrated.

The picture reminded me of the pictures of the Sacred Heart that were in homes when I was growing up. I also remembered prayers that sustained many people of the previous generation: 'Sacred Heart of Jesus I place my trust in you' and 'Jesus meek and humble of heart, make my heart like unto yours.' These prayers were a kind of 'mantra' for people, as they were repeated frequently during the day. They helped people to open their hearts to the love of the Sacred Heart of Jesus. They expressed trust in the love with which Jesus meets us when we come to him.

The following passage from John gives us an example of the love of the heart of Jesus:

> Mary went to Jesus, and as soon as she saw him she threw herself at his feet, saying, 'Lord, if you had been here, my brother would not have died.' At the sight of her tears, and those of the Jews who had come with her, Jesus was greatly distressed, and with a sigh that came straight from the heart he said, 'Where have you laid him?' They said, 'Lord, come and see.' Jesus wept; and the Jews said, 'See how he loved him!' (NJB, Jn: 11:32–36)

In St Matthew's Gospel we find a passage that conveys briefly but very movingly the compassion of Jesus for the suffering crowds. 'Jesus called his disciples to him and said: "I have compassion for the crowd, because they have been with me for three days now and have nothing to eat. I do not want to send them away hungry, or they might faint on the way"' (Mt 15:32) The miracle of the loaves follows.

In the Litany of the Sacred Heart, the heart of Jesus is described as a 'burning furnace of love' and as 'being pierced by a lance'. These expressions indicate that the love of the Sacred Heart is passionate and intense; there is nothing soft or sentimental about it. It is a love that was and is always gentle and humble, yet it is a love that led Jesus to endure the anguish of Gethsemane and a cruel and painful death on Calvary.

It is a love beyond all telling. It is love as compassion, which means to suffer with people and sacrifice oneself for others. This is the greatest love of all:

> Faith, which sees the love of God revealed in the pierced heart of Jesus on the cross, gives rise to love. Love is the light – and in the end, the only light – that can always illuminate a world grown dim, and give us the courage needed to keep living and working.[28]

⤜❧⤏

Christ's gaze purifies our hearts; the light of his countenance illumines the eyes of our hearts and teaches us to see everything in the light of his truth and his compassion for all people.[29]

6.2. A heart engaged with the 'little ones'

According to a conference in Dublin (2013) hosted by former president, Mary Robinson, the political and economic situation in some African countries is improving slightly. This does not take away from the fact that for many people on the continent life continues to be a dreadful struggle. None of the statistics or the harrowing pictures that we see on our TV screens can convey the deprivation and suffering that some people endure. The statistics beggar belief. Every year more than ten million children die in Africa of hunger and preventable diseases. In a Mill Hill sponsored primary school in western Kenya, well over one-third of the pupils are orphans and the number is increasing every year. Most of them are what they call 'AIDS Orphans' – since both parents have died of AIDS.

As of 2013, it is estimated that around twenty-four million people are infected with the HIV virus in sub-Saharan Africa – this is down around five million from where it was seven years ago. Many of these people will die, because they live in poverty and are destitute and malnourished. The drug therapy to keep them alive is becoming more available, but even if they get the therapy free, they often cannot afford good food and supplements that would keep them healthy and prolong life. They have little to look forward to, except a slow, painful and often lonely death – stigmatised because of the HIV infection. Individuals and families are devastated when a parent or both parents die. There are many widows with young children, and, when both parents have died, grandparents are often the only ones left to look after the orphaned children. These children are the lucky ones, as many orphans end up on the streets of the towns, fending for themselves.

In many situations, missionaries and aid workers are the eyes through which Christ's compassion looks at these people; they are the hands and feet of Christ as they try to help and comfort those in desperate need. As the missionaries experience it, suffering has a very human face. One of the most moving, compassionate pieces on this came from Bishop Kevin Dowling in South Africa:

When one looks into the eyes of a mother dying of AIDS, with a little child next to her who is also infected, the statistics become even more frightening in their poignancy and impact. Can we ever begin to imagine what is going on inside one of these 'little ones' – this little girl who watches as her mother gets more emaciated each day and fears that she is going to die ... But this is precisely what is required – as people, we need to enter the hearts and spirits of these 'little ones' and try to imagine what is happening inside, what they may be feeling as they struggle with poverty, hunger, fear of the future, and even basic questions like: will I have a place to stay? Will they take away our home when my mother dies?

Bishop Dowling's heart was engaged with the 'little ones' that he talked about. He is a great champion of AIDS victims and their families. This is the compassion of Christ at work in today's world. Compassion is the core of work with the poor and destitute. It awakens the human heart to those who suffer. I have seen missionaries and aid workers reach out to suffering humanity with dedication and commitment. Some of them do this for short periods, while others go on doing it for ten, twenty, thirty, forty, or even more years. Their hearts are truly engaged. They are the face and the heart of our compassionate Saviour for some of the poorest and most destitute people on earth.

⚭

Christ has no body now on earth but yours, no hands but yours, no feet but yours. Yours are the eyes through which Christ's compassion looks out on the world; yours are the feet with which he can go about doing good; yours are the hands with which he is to bless us now.
(St Teresa of Avila)

6.3. On a lonely road in Uganda

There are many people who, in the name of Jesus, go out with compassionate hearts to enter into the suffering of others and journey with them through their anguish. Their hearts go out to people who live in poverty and destitution, people who are victims of violence, war, corruption and exploitation. This can take people to extremes that can cost them their lives.

Every year the English Association for the Propagation of the Faith publishes a leaflet giving the names of Catholic missionaries murdered during the year. Two of my Mill Hill colleagues have been named on the leaflet. They were brutally murdered for speaking out in defence of innocent people. Fr Declan O'Toole from Headford, County Galway, was murdered in northern Uganda on 21 March 2002. Fr John Kaiser from the United States was murdered in Kenya on 24 August 2000.

Declan died on a lonely road in northern Uganda, far from his family and far from his home in County Galway. He was only thirty-one, having been ordained five years earlier at Claran, Headford. I met Declan for the last time in January of the year that he was murdered. We were both at a Mill Hill gathering in Kakamega, Kenya. He told me that he was finding life in Kotido (northern Uganda) very difficult. He also said that he sometimes feared that something could happen, but I doubt if he had any premonition about what would happen two months later, when he was shot dead on a dusty road in Kotido. He was travelling in a pick-up with two companions – the cook and catechist from the mission. Two soldiers stopped them and shot all three at point blank range. A short time later, the bodies were found seat-belted in the vehicle. Nothing had been taken or stolen from the car.

During his time in Kotido, Declan was very involved in development work and peacemaking. He wrote frequently about the insecurity in the area and about the many killings that were going on. He was very aware of the danger for missionaries working there. In the days leading up to the dreadful murders, Declan had spoken out against some army personnel who were mistreating the local people. This was happening to innocent people, as the Ugandan army was involved in a campaign to disarm local militia. Declan felt that there was an abuse of basic human rights and had reported this to the Irish ambassador in Kampala. He paid the ultimate price for his concern and compassion when he was shot dead a few days later.

Declan had a friendliness and gentleness about him that is rare. He was blessed with common sense and a sense of humour, and he was very spiritual. Initially, I found it hard to think of Declan as a martyr, because of the various things that the word conjures up. They seemed to belong to another age and to special people. But Declan was special. I now feel that he is in the company of people like Oscar Romero, who is described as a 'Martyr for Liberation'. Declan, at such a young age, is a martyr for the liberation of those defenceless people in northern Uganda. He is a martyr in the true sense of the word – a person of flesh and blood who was passionate about innocent people's rights. His concern was solidly grounded in Christ's compassion for suffering people. He was a true witness to Christ's love and presence in today's world, as his heart went out to those poor, defenceless people that he loved and served.

∝∾

Perhaps we are too used to thinking of the martyrs in rather distant terms, as though they were a category of the past, associated especially with the first centuries of the Christian era. The jubilee remembrance has presented us with a surprising vista, that our own time is particularly prolific in witnesses, who in different ways have lived the Gospel in the midst of hostility and persecution, often to the point of the supreme test of shedding their blood.
(Pope John Paul II)

6.4. On a lonely road in Kenya

Fr John Kaiser's name appeared on the list of missionaries who were murdered in the year 2000. John was another Mill Hill colleague. He died far from his family and his home in Minnesota, USA. His body was found under acacia trees on the side of the road near Naivasha – a town on the road from Nairobi to Nakuru. He had been shot through the head. John had been an outspoken critic of the brutal and corrupt government of President Daniel Arap Moi. He had spoken out about the abuse of human rights during tribal clashes and the land grabbing that went on for years. He was also outspoken on women's rights and the abuses that were taking place. In the months before his murder, he was harassed and hunted by powerful political figures. He knew he was in grave danger. He wrote: 'My life has been threatened. If I meet my death, then let it be. But let the people be given their rights.' To this he added:

> Since I have been threatened by the Rift Valley Commissioner, I want all to know that if I disappear from the scene, because the bush is vast and the hyenas many, that I am not contemplating any act of self destruction. Instead, I trust in a good guardian angel and in the action of grace. It is this same grace that can touch the minds and hearts of all.

John was a man of unwavering principles and great energy, as he fought for people's rights in his adopted country. He was fearless. The following quotation from the introduction to a book of his writings describes him well:

> With relentless courage and commitment, and moved by the compassion of Christ for human kind, John Kaiser pursued justice for poor victims. But, alas, he encountered a thick wall of official silence and intimidation by arrogant and powerful politicians. He began to receive death threats ... and his life was in danger ...

Then came the sad August morning when his body was found under acacia trees, brutally murdered. He suffered and died because of his compassion and care for the poor and suffering.

Soon after John's body was found, the Kenyan government, together with American FBI agents, came up with a report stating that John probably committed suicide. Nobody believed it. It took years for the truth to finally come out. Almost seven years later, to the day, came the announcement: 'Father John Kaiser was definitely murdered.' That was the verdict of a Nairobi court; one hundred and eleven witnesses testified during the hearings. The Nairobi Chief Magistrate Maureen Odero said that John Kaiser was definitely murdered.

Like Declan O'Toole, John died a martyr's death, martyred for the liberation of oppressed people, so that they may be given their rights. They were both murdered because they believed in the compassion of Christ and in his mission to bring hope and justice to some of the poorest and most oppressed people on the planet. Their deaths bring home to us the risks that people take for Christ and his people. Their lives were a living witness to the way Christ's 'heart goes out to all of these people'. Their courage and commitment has inspired many others to continue the struggle for a more just and peaceful world.

Declan and John both had a great passion for life and especially for the rights of innocent people. They knew they were living dangerously in challenging corrupt and brutal leaderships. They both knew that one side of loving has to do with ordinary daily living and with the way people relate to each other. But there is another side to love and compassion that can take one into dangerous situations that can lead to suffering and even death. This is the way it turned out for both of them. They were following in the footsteps of Jesus himself, who suffered and died for all. Their deaths are a reminder that the compassion of Jesus goes out to people in every age; it is gentle and humble, but it is also deep and passionate even to the point of death.

⁂

There are times when the burden of need and our own limitations might tempt us to become discouraged. But precisely then we are helped by the knowledge that, in the end, we are only instruments in the Lord's hands ...
To do all we can with what strength we have, however, is the task,
which keeps the good servant of Jesus Christ always at work:
'The love of Christ urges us on' (2 Cor 5:14).
(Pope Benedict: *God is Love*, 35)

6.5. The Spirit's presence

The early Christians adopted some elements of pagan paintings for use in a Christian context. There is a painting of Jesus as the 'Good Shepherd' on the ceiling of the catacomb of St Priscilla in Rome. It was painted in the second or third century and is one of the earliest paintings or representations of Jesus. It depicts Jesus carrying a sheep upon his shoulders, and standing in front of him are two sheep looking up at him and at the sheep that he is carrying. They symbolise the sheep of the fold welcoming back the lost sheep. It is obvious that the painting takes its inspiration from the stories in the New Testament about the good shepherd and the lost sheep. Jesus is the good shepherd, who goes in search of the lost sheep and lays down his life for his sheep. His heart goes out to all – with special care for the lost and lonely.

It is also likely that the painting owes something to pagan Roman culture. Many Roman tombs were decorated with paintings of Hermes (the ram-bearer) carrying a ram on his shoulders. Hermes was supposed to lead the souls of the deceased to the abode of the dead. In the paintings on pagan tombs, the ram's head is drooped because it is on its way to be sacrificed to the gods. In contrast, the sheep that Jesus is carrying is holding its head high as it is being welcomed back to the fold by the other sheep. Furthermore, the background in the painting of Jesus the good shepherd, with lots of green trees and enchanting birds, points to paradise, toward which the shepherd is leading his flock.

The painting is a good example of how the early Christians adopted a pagan image that dovetailed with the story of the good shepherd from the Gospels. As the early fathers of the Church saw it, the activity of the Spirit predisposed people and their cultures to receive the message of Jesus. Here, we are touching on a deep insight at the heart of Christian mission:

> The love of God, the Spirit of God, is present in people's hearts, in their history, in their culture and in their religion. The Holy Spirit, with its gifts, is there waiting for the person to awaken to the reality; the task is to discover those gifts, receive them with dialogue and foster them.[30]

Thus, the task of the missionary is to help people awaken to the reality of the Spirit and discover the presence of the Spirit's gifts, receive them with dialogue and foster them. In other words, the task of the missionary is to awaken people to God's abiding presence in their hearts and in their culture.

An image can help us here. When I was growing up we had an 'open fire' at home, and at night, when bedtime came, there were plenty of ashes and red hot coals. I remember well a little ritual that was repeated each night before we went to bed; it was a task reserved for an adult. My mother or father would bury the remains of the fire in ashes; the hot coals were carefully preserved in a bed of ashes and covered over with them. You could no longer see the fire or feel the heat; the glowing coals remained hidden overnight; they were referred to as 'griosach'.[31] The next morning the ashes were cleared away, the hot coals were rescued and a new fire was quickly started; soon the warmth, light and energy coming from the fire was there for all in the house to enjoy. When I worked in Kenya, I was surprised to find that some people there still preserve the fire in this way!

Like the fire hidden in the ashes, the spark of the divine (the Spirit) is alive in every human heart and in every culture. The warmth, light and energy of the Spirit may not be seen or felt until someone comes to foster an awareness of the Spirit. This is what mission is all about – awakening people to God's abiding presence and helping them to come to an awareness of Christ's Spirit present in their hearts. When we are involved in this delicate work of mission in the name of Jesus, heart speaks to heart. We are all called to be missionaries, to stir each other's hearts, to walk each other home.

∽

The fruit of the Spirit is love, joy, peace, patience, kindness, generosity, faithfulness, gentleness, and self-control … If we live by the Spirit, let us also be guided by the Spirit.
(Galatians 5:16–26)

6.6. Going out with love – mission and witness

The heart that is inspired by Christ wishes to go out and be involved in witness and service, mission and ministry. To be committed to Christ always implies the service of others and witnessing to the Good News by the lives we live, the example we give and the actions we risk taking. The African Synod document, *The Church in Africa*, explains it thus: 'The lesson of history confirms that by the action of the Holy Spirit, evangelisation takes place above all through the witness of charity, the witness of holiness ... every member of the faithful is called to holiness and called to mission' (136). It is also summed up in the encyclical *Redemptoris Missio*: 'The first form of evangelisation is witness', and witness is found in a life that manifests the 'unbreakable bond' between Christ's love for us and our love for others.

'To be called is to be sent' is a popular Swahili (Kenya) saying to describe the connection between being a follower of Christ and being his witness in today's world. We are all called to accept Christ's love, so that it can transform our hearts and affect our lives. We are called to be close to Christ to witness to his way in today's world. Jesus said to the disciples, 'As the Father has sent me, so I send you' (Jn 20:21) and, 'love one another. Just as I have loved you, you also should love one another. By this everyone will know that you are my disciples, if you have love for one another' (Jn 13:34–35).

Closeness to Christ is central to the life of the follower of Christ; the rest flows from it. The early Celtic missionaries were 'pilgrims for Christ' – they left home and country in order to be closer to Christ; it was the love of Christ and their seeking of Christ that was the impulse behind their going out as missionaries. Once they were in new countries they responded to the needs of those around them and conversions to Christ followed.

In the life of a Christian, the need for prayer and contemplation follows from the need to be close to Christ, to witness to his love and to be able to discern his Spirit present and active among those to whom we are sent. A contemplative style of missionary presence is very important. It means that the heart of the missionary is in tune with the heart of Jesus, the source of light and love – a heart that goes out to all people.

Our Mill Hill founder, Cardinal Herbert Vaughan, understood the connection between living the Christian life, witnessing and mission. He presented St Joseph as a model of missionary life. This is how it is expressed in the prologue to the Mill Hill Constitutions: Cardinal Vaughan 'pointed to St Joseph as a model of the apostolic (missionary) life, a model of steady quiet work, in an unusual faith situation, close to Jesus our Saviour and Mary his mother'.

The work of mission and witnessing often goes on quietly, with no great fanfare, far from the cameras and far from the spotlights. Fergal Keane, a distinguished foreign correspondent for the BBC for years, has reported from many countries in Africa and Asia. He has seen some awful human suffering and witnessed what missionaries are doing in the countries he visited time and again. His comment on the work of the missionaries and their way of doing things is given here in the quotation.

❦

I think that the missionaries who set out for Africa from Ireland in the 1950s and 60s, who went and lived in the villages with the local people and learned the local language and stayed there for years, well, there is something in what they did that a lot of latter-day would-be saviours of Africa with their 4x4s could do well to learn from.[32]

6.7. Young hearts go out to people

When she was in secondary school, Denise, one of my nieces, often said that she would like to go to Kenya with me to do voluntary work. She kept mentioning this while she was training as a teacher and during her first years of teaching. The day came when she travelled to Kenya with me in September 2006. She took up work as a volunteer helper for six months in the Pandipieri Catholic Centre in a slum area of Kisumu town. During her time there, she witnessed dreadful poverty and suffering, especially when she went with the community nurse, visiting sick people in their homes. This brought her face-to-face with the most appalling conditions in which people live.

From the funds that had been raised before she went to Kenya, she gave donations to various programmes run by Pandipieri Catholic Centre and by the sisters there. The programmes cater for street children, widows, orphans and needy families. Some money went into the alleviation of suffering and sickness through home-based healthcare programmes. She also donated money for school fees for street children and children from very poor families. On her visits to homes with the community nurse, she bought medicines, food, blankets, sheets, pillows and anything else that the nurse felt was needed.

Denise is just one of the young people who, over many years, have engaged generously with the poor and suffering in the slums of Kisumu. There were always helpers working at the Pandipieri Catholic Centre, most of them in their late teens and early twenties. They were deeply touched and affected by their experience of suffering humanity. Their hearts went out to the people that they came across. The presence of these young people is part of the changing face of mission. We are at the end of an era in terms of traditional missionary work, with the movement of people and funds from Europe through the various missionary congregations. This has meant so much to the people in mission lands, spiritually and materially. But missionaries are getting older and the numbers are decreasing rapidly.

In a letter to *The Irish Times* some years ago, John O'Shea, the founder of Goal summed it up:

In my thirty years of work in the developing world, I have not come across a better way of getting help to those who need it most, than through the missionaries on the ground. The disappearance en-masse of those 'on the missions' is an impending disaster for the developing world. Missionaries rarely make the headlines and are the forgotten heroes of the struggle for global equality. They are on the front line of development, literally saving lives. They left Ireland, not for career or profit, but for the relief of pain and suffering in some of the harshest terrain this earth has to offer.

I have no doubt that generous hearts will always be there to witness to the compassion of Christ, working for justice and engaging with the poor and suffering. Many groups are now involved in building homes, schools and orphanages in mission countries. People go for shorter periods but the commitment is there. These volunteers are touched by the plight of so many poor families and often moved to tears by what they see.

Those who work with the poor and oppressed can sometimes get discouraged. What is being done is so little in the face of the great sea of human suffering. Yet everything counts. Keeping one's eye and heart focused is important. Nothing is wasted. The Gospel assures us that the 'cup of water' or the 'welcome for a child' are openings for God's grace and have consequences way beyond anything we can know or imagine. Every small act that we perform is a little window for the love of Christ to touch the hearts of the poor and oppressed people that we go out to help.

⁖

How far that little candle throws its beams; so shines a good deed in a naughty world.
(Portia in Shakespeare's *Merchant of Venice*)

Be missionaries of God's love and tenderness and mercy.
(Pope Francis)

CHAPTER SEVEN

Open the Door of Your Heart

Open up the door of your heart;
let this Tremendous Lover into your being.
(Jean Vanier)

Let us swing wide all the doors and windows
of our hearts on their rusty hinges
So that we may learn how to open in love.
(Dawna Markova)

7.1. Opening the heart to God's love

'Heart speaks unto heart' was the motto of Blessed John Henry Newman. Pope Benedict XVI said that the motto 'gives us an insight into Cardinal Newman's understanding of the Christian life as a call to holiness, experienced as the profound desire of the human heart to enter into intimate communion with the heart of God'. We enter this communion when our human hearts are opened and awakened by an experience of love that flows from the heart of God. And God's love, God's voice, comes as an invitation:

> God's voice in this world is never coercive or overbearing in any way, but is always an invitation and a beckoning that respects you and your freedom ... God's voice judges us not by overpowering us, but by shining love and light into all those places where we find ourselves huddled in fear, shame, bitterness, hostility and sin ... We need to view God, always, as non-coercive ... God's voice invites, beckons, leaves you free, and is as non-threatening as the innocence and powerlessness of a baby – or a saint ... Too often, however sincerely we might be doing this, the voice we try to give to God is too laden with coercion, threat, manipulation, violence, harshness, our own judgments, our own fears, our own wounds and especially our own egos, to bear enough resemblance to the divine kenosis [self-emptying] and free invitation that Jesus gave voice to in his birth, life and message ...[33]

Through his experience of conversion, St Augustine discovered that God's love invites and beckons. He talked about 'being drawn by the bonds of love that only lovers would understand'. He also said, 'God sets the heart on fire with love of God and neighbour and is himself that love.' He felt that God is close upon the heels of those who run away from Him.

He saw the experience of God's love as the driving force in our quest for God and our encounter with God. It is love that motivates a person through all the inner change that comes about when the heart is touched and awakened. This inner change is called conversion, repentance – a change of heart or perhaps a move to the heart, so that 'heart speaks unto heart'.

Augustine was convinced of God's search for the sinner and that the experience of God's love makes a change of heart possible. He knew from experience that when his own heart was touched and awakened to God's presence and love, he was able to turn his aimless wandering through life into a pilgrimage deep into the mystery of God.

A question to reflect on: what can I do to open my heart to God's love and respond to it in my life? Perhaps this little story can give some help and guidance:

> A disciple asked a spiritual guide, 'Is there anything I can do to gain holiness?'
>
> 'As little as you can do to make the sun rise in the morning,' was the response.
>
> 'Then what is the use of all the spiritual exercises?' the disciple enquired.
>
> 'To make sure,' the master said, 'that you are not asleep when the sun begins to rise.'

There is a deep insight here. We can express it in this way: while we can do something with prayer and spiritual exercises to open our hearts to God's love, we cannot make it happen, nor do we have to. God first loves us and invites us to receive his love, experience it, live it and share it with others. God's love for us is certain as the dawn and the sunrise. And we are advised to be awake to make sure that we are ready and open to receive God's love, when it is poured into our hearts through the Holy Spirit given to us (Rom 5:5).

⤜⤙

My heart is steadfast, O God, my heart is steadfast.
I will sing and make melody.
Awake, my soul! Awake, O harp and lyre! I will awake the dawn.
(Ps 57 7–8)

7.2. 'Perfect love casts out fear'

Michael Paul Gallagher describes an experience he once had:

> On the way back something happened at the railway bridge: just four steps from the bottom stood three women, two youngish and the third elderly and frail. The old lady suddenly addressed me. It was not clear what she was saying but the gist was to ask me to stand there and catch her if she were to fall. She had already come down some fifteen steep steps, but had now suddenly lost her nerve and got stuck. For some reason she had more confidence in the stranger at the foot of the stairs than in her two (as I imagine) daughters. So I stopped and watched as she successfully descended the remaining steps. She waved a thank you. How easy it is to lose confidence and how easy to restore it.[34]

This is so true: it is easy to lose confidence and it is easy to restore it – sometimes. I use the word 'sometimes' as we all know that emotional problems with confidence and fear can run deep. There can be serious problems from a lack of confidence, lack of acceptance and lack of love. This is when fear and anxiety invade people's hearts in a major way, and run through their lives like a tsunami that can cause endless pain and suffering. This crippling fear and anxiety can be a real obstacle to opening one's heart to God's presence and love.

Many people carry a heavy cross of personal, physical and emotional suffering. It can be any debilitating physical illness that goes on for years. Much suffering is hidden, silent, almost secret. This is especially true for those who suffer great emotional pain. Some people have to live with fear and anguish, darkness and distress, much of their lives. They cannot get away from the anxiety and fear that invades their hearts. This can be rooted in the experiences of childhood, when there was a lack of love and acceptance. Fr Piet van Breemen puts it this way:

> Every human being craves to be accepted, accepted for what he or she is. Nothing in human life has such a lasting and fatal effect as the experience of not being completely accepted. When I am not accepted then something in me is broken. A baby who is not welcome is ruined at the roots of his or her existence.[35]

Love and acceptance provide the atmosphere in which we can grow and develop and be ourselves. We cannot grow unless we are drawn out by the warm touch of another. We cannot open the door of the heart by ourselves. Most of us are lucky enough to have found love in our family life – though of course there is no perfect family. In the ordinary ups and downs of life, we pick up some emotional scars but hopefully there was enough love and acceptance to save us from the more serious ones. Unfortunately, this is not always the case. Some people are locked into negativity and inner darkness that is not of their own making. It can take years of effort and much help, sometimes professional help, to unravel the complex roots of the fear and anxiety that such people experience.

Christ calls us to love God with all our hearts and to love others as we love ourselves. While loving others can prove difficult, loving 'self' can be even more of a challenge when the bad experiences of the past have left one with deep emotional scars and a fearful heart. Crippling fear makes it more difficult to open the door of the heart to God, self and others. Yet we are assured that the spiritual journey is the story of the human heart (often fearful and anxious) awakening to the mystery of a loving God, who reaches out to us and draws us into his loving embrace. This is a God who loves us so much that he sent his only Son into the world so that we can be saved and redeemed from all the darkness, fear and negativity that invades our hearts and lives: 'There is no fear in love; perfect love casts out fear' (1 Jn 4:18). We recall here the father's welcome and embrace for the prodigal son that casts out his fears.

∽

Do not let your hearts be troubled or afraid,
trust in God and trust in me.
(Jn 14:1)

Lord, when the cares of my heart are many,
your consolations cheer my soul.
(Ps 94:19)

7.3. 'Facing the dragon'

In the 1970s, soon after my ordination, I found myself in Chicago studying spirituality. It was a daunting experience at first, far from home in a big city where I knew nobody. Gradually, I settled in and it turned out to be a rewarding time for me. One of the staff, Robert L. Moore, gave me a lot of help and encouragement. He was a lecturer in psychology, but he was also interested in mythology, theology, spirituality and other subjects.

I have kept an eye out for his books ever since. There is one in particular that I find very interesting. The title is: *Facing the Dragon – Confronting personal and spiritual grandiosity*.[36] As the subtitle suggests, he asserts that each of us is born with an innate grandiosity. The dragon is an image used in mythology for this grandiosity. Many of us, if not all, have fantasies about ourselves that exaggerate our own importance. This can manifest itself in the impressions that we give to others and that we have of ourselves. We may feel that we know everything, that we are always right, that we are in control of things, that others should listen and obey – the list is endless. Behind all these fantasies there can sometimes be a larger fantasy that we are God!

As Moore sees it, personal grandiosity is the source of greed, ambition, bitterness, hostility, rage and resentment. From these flow many of the personal and social problems, and the violence and war between individuals, peoples and nations. He also says that the failure to recognise this grandiosity is very dangerous. The modern fantasy, he writes, believes that we are better off without God and the churches, but that fantasy does not take into account the rise of a culture that is narcissistic and full of harmful grandiosity.

For Moore, the resources for confronting grandiosity might surprise us – seeing that he is a professional psychologist. Among the resources, he lists: regular participation in worship and liturgy; belonging to a religious community or to a group like Alcoholics Anonymous; having ritual symbols such as a rosary or crucifix, and especially a life of prayer. He notes:

> This recommendation of prayer is perhaps the most radical. I can hear people gasping: 'My God – is a professional psychoanalyst going to recommend prayer?' Yes, in fact, I am ... There is a body

of research that shows how prayer can be helpful in both emotional and physical health.

For him, and for us, prayer helps to open our hearts to God's abiding presence and love in such a way that we become more aware of our grandiosity and remember that we ourselves are creatures and not God. We are human beings remarkably blessed with divine love flowing through our veins if we open our hearts to receive it.

We can express this in language that is more familiar to us. Grandiosity has a lot in common with pride and pretentiousness, and prayer is our most important resource as we face the dragon – pride. Prayer leads to growth in self-knowledge that keeps us humbly aware that we are indeed like the rest of men and women – in need of redemption. Humility is the willingness to open our hearts to the mystery of God and to our own human limitations and need for God. For Richard Rohr, the only worthy response before the awesome mystery of God is humility. Humility is the wisdom of the heart that helps us to live our lives in a way that is open to God's presence so that we can 'let this tremendous lover into our being'. The tax collector had humility and went home at peace with God, while the Pharisee did not, because his pride kept his heart closed to God's love. This is what pride and grandiosity do. Humility does the opposite – it keeps us searching and open to God's love, life, truth and forgiveness.

Pride is something that we have to confront if we want to open up the door of the heart to God's love, and 'let this tremendous lover into our being'.

❧

If we are like the Pharisee who said: 'Thank you, Lord, for not making me like all the other men, and especially not like that publican'… well, then we do not know the heart of the Lord, and we shall never have the joy of feeling his mercy. God is ready to embrace us … let us take up God's offer.
(Pope Francis)

7.4. A humble disposition

For Robert Moore, grandiosity (pride) is the source of much personal and social evil in the world. It is the source of many of our vices. It is like a lock that keeps the door of the heart closed to the healing power and loving presence of God. As a result, mean and nasty things come from inside us and are manifest in our behaviour. All this is lived out at a practical, personal level in the way we relate to others and the way we feel about ourselves.

Humility, on the other hand, is like a doorstopper that keeps the door of the heart open to God's love and mercy, goodness and truth. It has been described as the mother of many virtues. It is like the glue that holds the other virtues together. To use a present day image, we could say it is the 'Higgs Boson' particle that was recently discovered in physics, which holds other particles together. Interestingly, the 'Higgs Boson' is sometimes referred to as the 'God particle' – much to the annoyance of scientists!

The word 'humility' has often been misused, and sometimes still is; to be humble meant putting oneself down. C. S. Lewis wrote:

> Do not imagine that when you meet a really humble man he will be what most people call humble nowadays: he will not be a sort of person who is always telling you that, of course, he is nobody. Probably all you will think about him is that he seemed a cheerful, intelligent person, who took a real interest in what you said to him ... He will not be thinking about humility; he will not be thinking about himself at all.

The humble person has an ease about himself or herself, because of a degree of healthy self-knowledge and an awareness of the closeness of God who is good, loving and forgiving. Self-knowledge brings awareness of faults and failings, and of the need for God's healing mercy and forgiveness. Thus humility awakens the heart and opens it to God.

Humility and pride are lived out every day before our eyes in interpersonal relationships. The Irish writer, Frank O' Connor, captured this very well in a short story entitled: *My First Confession*.[37] It belongs to the Ireland of the past, but it is still interesting – and even amusing! Despite the fact that it is dated, the story fits in with what Robert Moore recommends in terms of resources to help us face the dragon – pride. Moore does not mention confession, but he is very positive about groups that give people an opportunity to humbly admit their faults and failings.

Frank O'Connor's story deals with humility and pride, but also touches on other areas such as one's image of God and sense of sin and guilt.

In the story, we read that Jackie was weighed down with 'the crimes of a lifetime', as he headed for his first confession. He felt he had broken each of the Ten Commandments and felt he was lost. Even Nora his sister didn't know the half of what he had to tell, if he told it. He was in a terrible state of fear and anxiety. Nora's constant teasing had not helped matters. He said that she had ways of getting at him that nobody else knew about. But the real trouble was much deeper.

The teacher had drilled the fear of Hell into him with stories of what happened to people who died having made a bad confession. These stories shocked him and affected him deeply. He ended up with a fear of God, an exaggerated sense of sin and was burdened with excessive guilt. To add to his misery, on the way to confession Nora tormented him:

> Oh, God help us. Isn't it a terrible pity you weren't a good boy? Oh, Jackie, my heart bleeds for you! How will you ever think of all your sins? … I don't know what the priest will do with you at all, Jackie. He might have to send you to the bishop.

To Jackie's great surprise, the confession was a good experience. It turned out to be a great release for him. He found he could talk to the priest and got on well with him. His fear quickly disappeared and the sense of foreboding that haunted him prior to confession soon melted away. He left the church in great spirits, feeling at ease with himself, at peace with God and delighted to have 'one up on Nora'!

⌒☙⌒

Let us lie down again
deep in anonymous humility and God
may find us worthy material for His hand.
('Having Confessed' by Patrick Kavanagh)

7.5. ''Tis no advantage to anybody trying to be good'

As Frank O'Connor's story continues, we read that while Nora let on to be an angel, Jackie knew well that this was not the case, as she constantly teased and tormented him. When Nora's turn for confession came, Jackie heard her voice, as if butter wouldn't melt in her mouth! When she came out, her eyes were lowered, her head was bowed and her hands were joined. She walked up the aisle to the side altar, looking like a saint. Jackie had never seen such an exhibition of devotion. Later we find the same Nora sticking out her tongue at Jackie behind the priest's back!

After confession, the priest walked out of the church with Jackie. Nora was sitting on the small wall outside the church, waiting for him. She put on a very sour face when she saw the priest with him:

'Well,' she asked coldly, after he left me, 'what did he give you?'

'Three Hail Marys,' I said.

'Three Hail Marys,' she repeated incredulously. 'You mustn't have told him anything.'

'I told him everything,' I said confidently.

'About Gran and all?'

'About Gran and all.'

(All she wanted was to be able to go home and say I'd made a bad confession.)

'Did you tell him you went for me with the bread-knife?' she asked with a frown.

'I did to be sure.'

'And he only gave you three Hail Marys?'

'That's all.'

She slowly got down from the railing with a baffled air. Clearly, this was beyond her. As we mounted the steps back to the main road, she looked at me suspiciously.

'What are you sucking?' she asked.

'Bullseyes.'

'Was it the priest gave them to you?'

''Twas.'

'Lord God,' she wailed bitterly, 'some people have all the luck! 'Tis no advantage to anybody trying to be good. I might just as well be a sinner like you.'

Of course, it is only a story, but we are left to wonder if this was the beginning of growth in self-knowledge for Nora that would leave her more humble and open. From what she said, she obviously felt she was being good and she was intensely annoyed that Jackie the sinner is delighted with himself. As far as she was concerned, there was no justice. But, of course, it is not that simple; it is not easy to tell who is the sinner and who is being good. Much of what we do is affected by how we see ourselves, others and God. Our attitudes and inner dispositions are crucial. Pride can be deeply rooted and the journey to humility can be slow and difficult.

Frank O'Connor's short story challenges us to look deeper into our hearts. It opens up questions about the delusions we can have about others and especially about ourselves. It points out the dangers of pride and the need for humility. It shows that there are traces of pride in all of us; Jackie was not immune – he was delighted to have one up on Nora! The story also brings home to us the amount of fear that is often present in our faith and in our idea (picture) of God.

Fortunately, much has changed since the story was written. The younger generation today is spared most of the excesses that instilled such a fear of God – and fear of making a bad confession! There is now a welcome stress on a loving God, a Father who is fond of us and embraces us and is ready to forgive and heal us, a Saviour who died for us: 'See what love the Father has given us' (1 Jn 3:1).

For many of us of an earlier generation, the story brings back memories of how it used to be. The fear and worry can still be very real. It can take years to break away from the false images of God that affect us. It takes time to realise that we carry the burden of sin in the presence of a gracious merciful God, as we try to open our hearts to his light, love and peace.

⋘⋙

God always waits for us, even when we have left him behind!
He is never far from us, and if we return to him, he is ready to embrace us …
let us take up God's offer – his caress of love … Mercy is the Lord's most
powerful message …

The confessional must not be a torture chamber, but an encounter with the
Lord's mercy which spurs us on to do our best.

Argue as much as you want; if the plates start flying, so be it. But never let
the day end without making peace – never!
(Pope Francis)

7.6. Discernment – a key to the door

Discernment is a key to open up the door of your heart, and 'let this tremendous lover into your being'. Discernment keeps us attentive to the promptings of the Spirit of God so that the Spirit can lead us and we can live a life in the Spirit.

The image of a sailing ship can help us to understand how the Spirit of God works in us. Try to imagine a sailing ship helplessly drifting with the current at the mouth of the harbour. It is waiting for a breeze. Then it comes, a powerful wind fills the limp and lifeless sails. The ship begins to move slowly and then with some speed. Soon it is headed out into the open sea, leaving the safety of the harbour well behind. It powers its way out into the deep ocean. And so it is with us. The Spirit fills our sails and powers us forward on our journey into the mystery of God. But too often our wilfulness takes hold of us and we strive with all our might to follow our own will, resisting the prompting and power of the Spirit.

Discernment helps us to notice the various ways in which the Spirit of God is present and active. It can be described as 'feeling our way with insight'. It is focused on human experience and is found in a discerning heart. The key aspects of discernment are: noticing, perceiving, feeling, inner movement and the inner life, while all sorts of external matters in life and relationships are also relevant, as well as theology, scripture and the tradition.

St Ignatius used the Spanish word 'sentir' when he described discernment. John Futrell writes:

> In the process of discernment, 'sentir' comes to mean above all a kind of felt-knowledge, an affective, intuitive knowledge possessed through the reaction of human feelings to exterior and interior experience. Thus, discernment involves felt-knowledge that is affective and intuitive.[38]

This indicates that the heart is central in discernment, but the word 'intuitive' (to perceive with insight) indicates that the head too has its place. A phrase sums it up: 'Trust your heart but also use your head.'

Growth in love is the clearest indication that we are being 'led by the Spirit'. St Paul brings this out very clearly. He says that if he has all the gifts of men and of angels and has faith to move mountains, even if he would give his body to be burnt, but has no love, then he is just a gong booming and a symbol clashing (1 Cor 13). So growth in the love of Christ is the clearest and possibly the only real indication that we are moving in the right direction. Furthermore, love of others is the true manifestation of our love of Christ: 'The truth of our union with Jesus Christ in the Eucharist is tested by whether or not we love our fellow men and women; it is tested by how we treat others' (Pope John Paul II).

A deepening of Christian faith and love is the foundation for discernment, which is something that helps us to feel our way on our journey into the mystery of God. The habit of discernment is a key that opens the door of the heart to let 'this tremendous lover into your being'.

A discerning heart knows that anything that leads to hatred, bitterness, hostility and confusion is not from God, and anything that produces the fruits of the Spirit in a person's life comes from God – the fruits of the Spirit being: 'Love, joy, peace, patience, kindness, generosity, faithfulness, gentleness, self-control' (Gal 5:22).

⸎

You will know them by their fruits. Are grapes gathered from thorns or figs from thistles? In the same way, every good tree produces good fruit and a rotten tree bad fruit. A good tree cannot bear bad fruit, nor can a bad tree bear good fruit ... you will know them by their fruits ...
(Mt 7:16–20)

7.7. God's weird and wonderful ways

In October 2011, the doctor told me that I had prostate cancer. The news of the cancer came as a shock. The word 'cancer' always has a chilling sound to it that raises fears and anxieties. It helped me to be told that the cancer was being picked up in time and that there is a high recovery rate with prostate cancer. Many people have to cope with much worse news about other types of cancer.

The evening before the surgery, I was walking around the hospital, feeling fine physically, but anxious about the operation in the morning. I visited the chapel in the hospital and sat there for a while. When I stood up to leave, a small leaflet on one of the chairs caught my eye. There was a picture of a lovely sunset on it. I picked it up and looked at it. I turned it over and there was a verse of a Psalm, which read: 'Be strong, and let your heart take courage, all you who wait for the Lord' (Ps 31:24). I sat down again and spent a while looking at the sunset and reflecting on the verse. The words 'Be strong' and 'take courage' together with the words 'hope in God' were comforting. I felt some of the anxiety leave me. It is amazing how something small can make a difference – sometimes. That little text became very important to me in the days, weeks and months that followed. I found myself repeating it often, and had my own variations of it to make a short prayer: 'Lord, let my heart find courage [I would also use other words: comfort, strength, peace, rest, love] as I place all my hope in you.' I found these short prayers helpful, especially when I did not feel like or able to pray around the time of the surgery and during the period of recovery. As you may know only too well, it can be difficult to pray when one is ill. And some of the language that God hears when someone is suffering may not be very polite! We find this in the Psalms.

While I was good immediately after the surgery and the doctor was happy with the way things went, I went through two nights where I slept very little and during the day I felt weak and sore. I remember looking around the room in the hospital and having strange feelings; I was not feeling myself. I soon realised that major surgery takes its toll, not only physically, but also emotionally. The body suffers its trauma and so too does the soul, the spirit, the heart, the self. The word 'ambushed' came to mind – I was in 'good health' two days earlier and now on the flat of my back, feeling sore, weak and helpless. I remembered something from Africa: among some African tribes, people believe that when a person is seriously hurt physically or emotionally, the soul or spirit moves some distance away from the body. The more brutal the hurt, the greater the distance the soul moves away. They also believe that the soul will only return when it is coaxed back ever so gently with great love, care and affection.

I will always be grateful to the surgeon and would never accuse him of 'ambushing' me, but surgery is invasive and while the purpose is to get a person back to health, the experience and its aftermath are traumatic. As the days passed in the hospital, I began to feel better. Using the African image, I can say that the hospital staff, my family, friends and Mill Hill colleagues were coaxing my soul and body back together and back to health.

A friend sent me this note a few weeks after the surgery: 'May you quickly get going, now, Jim, without further treatments, and all the better for your unexpected time off. It will have deepened your spirit – in God's weird ways of doing such things.' Yes, in God's weird and wonderful ways, the human spirit can be deepened and the human heart awakened to God's presence through suffering and setbacks in life. But it is also easy to lose heart. Some people become bitter when suffering comes their way, so it is a real blessing if we can hope in a loving God and not get discouraged. It is often an answer to our own prayers and the prayers of others.

⌘

Be strong, let your heart take courage, all you who hope in God.
(Ps 31:24)

God hovers in love over the fragments of our brokenness. Over the dark and storm-tossed waters, God hovers in mercy.
(St Augustine)

CHAPTER EIGHT

The Landscape of a Loving Heart

Keep your gaze fixed upon Jesus; in him all the anguish and all the longing of the human heart finds fulfilment.
(Pope Francis)

8.1. One man's remarkable journey

As a ten-year-old boy from the Catholic Creggan Estate in Derry, Richard Moore was on his way home from school in 1972, when he was seriously injured. A soldier fired a rubber bullet that struck him on the bridge of his nose, leaving him with the most awful facial injuries that led to the loss of his sight in both his eyes. His life was changed forever.

Richard, one of a family of twelve, tells his story in the fascinating book: *Can I Give Him My Eyes?* The title of the book came from the question Richard's father asked the doctors when they broke the news that they could not save Richard's sight.[39] In the book, Richard tells a truly remarkable story about the tragedy that befell him, but also about courage, forgiveness, acceptance and the triumph of the human spirit over great adversity. It gives deep insights into Richard's journey to having a loving heart that was able to forgive and befriend the solider who fired the rubber bullet. It also describes how Richard has dedicated his life to helping children caught up in the horrors of war. He set up an organisation called Children in Crossfire, which is helping children in many different countries.

How was Richard able to accept blindness and cope with it? How was he able to forgive and befriend the soldier who fired the rubber bullet? And how was he able to put his life back together? He writes:

> The simplest answer is my parents and their strong faith. It was their total lack of bitterness ... I used to say it was because I was lucky, but that is not so; luck had nothing to do with it. It was, quite simply, that I was blessed – blessed by the power of my parents' prayers. I genuinely believe it was the devotion of my mammy and my daddy and their prayers that ultimately helped me to have such a positive and enjoyable life. Otherwise it is inexplicable.

Richard explains how he became friends with Charles, the soldier who fired the rubber bullet that blinded him. After initial suspicion between them, they gradually moved on to become friends:

One of the principle factors in helping me to cope with blindness was forgiveness. That I harboured no hatred towards the soldier who shot me, or towards the British Army, freed me from the burden of bitterness. That I forgave the solider meant I wasn't carrying that baggage through my life. It left me free to deal with other things and with the practical issues around blindness, such as mobility and developing the necessary skills for the future. Acceptance was also very important in dealing with blindness.

He goes on to say that the process of forgiveness does not change the past:

By forgiving the solider, I am not going to get my eyesight back, but forgiveness can change the future, and that is what happened in my case.

He also writes about bitterness and anger:

When I thought about bitterness and anger, I could see they were self-destructive emotions that would affect no one but me. Like a cancer, they would have destroyed me from the inside out … Anything that I have achieved in life, I believe, I would not have achieved had I allowed anger and bitterness to be the dominant forces.

Richard's truly remarkable story is one of the most powerful testimonies to love and forgiveness that I have come across. He offers deep insights into the journey one travels to reach a loving, forgiving heart that is free of hatred, anger and bitterness. The loving hearts of his parents were central to that journey. Their faith and their total lack of bitterness helped Richard to cope with his blindness. He felt he was blessed by the power of their prayers and devotion.

⸺

Those who refuse to forgive break the bridge which they themselves must cross.
(A proverb)

8.2. Open to God's mercy

A loving heart comes with an awakening to God's presence and an experience of God's mercy. This happens when we are aware of our sinfulness, but we also know and believe that we are sinners loved by God. In the parable of the Pharisee and the Tax Collector, the Pharisee had no awareness of his pride and lack of charity. The tax collector, on the other hand, was aware that he was a sinner but had a sense that God loved him. This was his salvation. He prayed with a contrite, humble heart, not even daring to raise his eyes to heaven: 'Lord, be merciful to me, a sinner.' He was filled with sorrow for his sins and his heart was open to receive God's forgiveness. This is the way to a change of heart (conversion, repentance). He went home at peace with God – with love in his heart.

As Jesus presents it, mercy and forgiveness flow from the heart of God. In his preaching, John the Baptist called people to repentance because of the judgement that was approaching. With Jesus we have a different emphasis. Jesus preached repentance, but before that, he proclaimed that the kingdom of God is here; in other words, the forgiveness and love of God is being revealed in Jesus himself (Mk 1:15). Jesus reveals God as a merciful father who welcomes the sinner home, as a good shepherd who searches for the lost sheep, and as a woman who goes to great trouble searching for the lost coin.

Among the last words of Jesus on the cross, in the midst of his anguish, we find mercy and forgiveness: 'Father, forgive them; for they do not know what they are doing' (Lk: 23:34). These words have deep significance. Far too often, doubts are sown in our minds and hearts about the forgiveness that flows from the heart of Jesus. It is only through the experience of his forgiveness that we are able to forgive. Such an experience touches the heart and leaves us with a loving heart that seeks and grants forgiveness.

We can learn so much about God's mercy from the story of the prodigal son and the merciful father. The first part of the story portrays God's gracious forgiveness of the prodigal son. The sinner was warmly welcomed and reinstated without condition. The second focuses on the other son, the righteous one, who was hurt and scandalised. It is not fair! This was his mistake; he had not understood that God's sense of forgiveness is not fair! God is wholly merciful and boundless in his forgiveness. This even outweighs our sense of fairness and justice. The father who had embraced the younger son is gentle too with the aggrieved elder son: 'Son, you are always with me, and all that is mine is yours.' He is in no way worse off because the father is merciful and forgiving. What is in question is recognition of a merciful father and, ultimately, a merciful God.[40]

There was a story in the early Church claiming that it was the mother who sent a message secretly to the prodigal son and was mainly responsible for his return. Her message went something like this:

> Son, just know that if you feel like coming home, nobody will say anything to you. If you feel as bad as I suspect you do, you have punished yourself quite enough – the older people say that sin brings its own punishment? You have gone through enough already. Maybe you feel you have to earn our love. You don't; we love you not because you are good or bad, but because you are our son and nothing can change that. Home is not where you live, it is where you are loved and belong.

∽

It is not easy to trust oneself to the mercy of God, because His mercy is an unfathomable abyss – but we must do it. God has the ability to forget … He kisses you, He embraces you, and He says to you: 'Neither do I condemn you. Go, and from now on, sin no more.' Only that counsel does He give you. We ask for the grace of never tiring of asking pardon, for He never tires of pardoning.

(Pope Francis)

8.3. 'Wrapped in compassionate awareness'

The journey to a loving heart can be long and difficult. Yet it is the road we travel if we want to become 'safe sacraments of divine forgiveness' – wrapped in 'compassionate awareness of others'.

There is an English expression, 'Unforgiving, Unforgiven', that highlights the very close connection between our ability to receive forgiveness from God and our willingness to forgive others. We pray in the Our Father: 'Forgive us our trespasses, as we forgive those who trespass against us.' In trying to be more loving and forgiving, most of us have to make a real effort. You may be one of the lucky ones who are forgiving by nature, but many people are not normally this way. It depends a lot on our upbringing. We can be kind-hearted when it does not cost us too much or when it is to our advantage. We are often far too self-centred to love and forgive easily. It can be a struggle to act kindly and lovingly towards others – with compassionate awareness and forgiveness. It is little short of a miracle to be able to forgive when one has been badly hurt and damaged.

Nelson Mandela continually reminded his fellow prisoners in South Africa that unless they let go of their hurts they would remain in the grip of their oppressors. Dr Sheila Cassidy, who was tortured in South America, had this to say:

> I would never say to someone: 'you must forgive'. I would not dare. Who am I to tell a woman whose father abused her, or a mother whose daughter has been raped, that she must forgive? I can only say: however much we have been wronged, however justified our hatred, if we cherish it, it will poison us. We must pray for the power to forgive, for it is in forgiving that we are healed.

The following gem of a passage comes from Daniel O'Leary; it is about the kind of people who are 'safe sacraments of divine forgiveness'. It is a description of what we mean by a forgiving heart that is wrapped in compassionate awareness of others. He says it is very important to understand forgiveness not as repeated acts, out of duty or for eternal reward, whether seven times or seventy-seven times, but to see forgiveness as being about 'becoming and being a forgiving person all of the time':

It is about being permanently wrapped in the grace of compassionate awareness of others, in general, or of another human being in particular, in whom war is being waged between the forces of light and darkness; of understanding the precariousness and fragility of sanity and of the infinite and bewildering complexity of the human spirit ... It is only those familiar with the ambiguity of their own strange contradictions and paradoxes of inner and outer behaviour, who are safe sacraments of divine forgiveness. Such people will never judge or condemn. Their self-aware hearts are too wise. 'To know all,' wrote St Antoine Exupery, as he realised with shocking clarity in the despair of the desert, 'is to forgive all'. Such are the times when we allow the rainbows of heaven to break through the mists of earth.[41]

A suggestion here: Try to be aware, deeply and compassionately aware, of the strange contradictions and paradoxes of your own inner and outer behaviour. How does one develop such awareness? One of the ways open to us is prayer, especially silent prayer.

❧

Nowhere so much as in the practice of forgiveness am I made so aware of my sinfulness, my selfishness ... Perceptive, quick to see the flaws in another, I was prone to criticism, finding a certain satisfaction in seeing another at fault ... I realised I had the mentality of a Pharisee but, I thought to myself, if the Pharisee had turned to Our Lord and admitted his hardness of heart, his crabbed mean spirit, and asked for help, Our Lord would have helped him. So I did the same ... I realised that charity and forgiveness must begin in the heart, and so I tried to think kindly and lovingly (with compassionate awareness!) of others.
(Ruth Burrows, Carmelite sister)

8.4. A gentle and humble heart

There is an ancient story about *The Wind and the Sun* (Aesop's Stories: 620–560 BC). It goes like this:

> Once upon a time when everything could talk, the Wind and the Sun fell into an argument as to which was the stronger. Finally, they decided to put the matter to a test; they would see which one could make a certain man, who was walking along the road, take off his overcoat. The Wind tried first, and began to blow and blow. The harder and colder the wind blew, the tighter the traveller wrapped his overcoat about him. The Wind finally gave up, and told the Sun to try. The Sun began to smile and as it grew warmer and warmer, the man was comfortable once more. But the Sun shone brighter and brighter until the man grew too hot, and started sweating. He first opened his coat and this gave him some relief. But that lasted only for a while, as the Sun grew still warmer. He soon stopped and removed his overcoat. He then sat on a stone and placed the overcoat on the ground beside him. The Sun was declared the winner. The gentle warmth of the Sun accomplished what the cold harsh Wind could not do.

The moral of this story is that gentleness and warmth are far more effective than harshness and force. For the Christian, the message is similar; a loving heart is gentle and warm:

> Love is patient; love is kind; love is not envious or boastful or arrogant or rude. It does not insist on its own way; it is not irritable or resentful; it does not rejoice in wrongdoing, but rejoices in the truth. It bears all things, believes all things, hopes all things, endures all things. (1 Cor 13:4–7)

Jesus himself is the best example of such a loving heart. He could be firm and fearless, as he was when he cleared the sellers from the Temple and when he confronted the Pharisees. But he was gentle and humble in his dealings with his disciples and others, especially with sinners. He had a special care for the lost, the sick, the lonely and the oppressed, and his gentleness was there for all to see.

In one of the most comforting verses in the New Testament, Jesus referred to the gentleness of his own heart: 'Come to me, all you that are weary and are carrying heavy burdens, and I will give you rest. Take my yoke upon you, and learn from me; for I am gentle and humble in heart, and you will find rest for your souls' (Mt 11:28–30). There is much comfort in these words of Jesus. It is one of the few places where he speaks about his own heart. He does so to reveal the humility and gentleness with which he greets us when we come to him, especially when we are struggling with the burdens and bleak times in life.

St John Bosco worked wonders in his ministry to youth and also to prisoners and those on the margins of society. Towards the end of his life, reflecting on many years' experience, he wrote these words about how to win over people and lead them to Christ:

> Meekness [gentleness] was the method that Jesus used with the apostles. He put up with their ignorance and roughness and even their infidelity. He treated sinners with a kindness and affection that caused some to be shocked, others to be scandalised, and still others to hope for God's mercy. And so he bade us to be gentle and humble of heart.

❦

May the God of gentleness be with you, caressing you with sunlight, rain and wind.
May his tenderness shine through you to warm all those who are hurt and lonely.
May the blessing of gentleness be upon you.
(An Irish blessing)

8.5. A horizon of hope

I remember seeing an unusual poster some years ago. There was a photo of a dog standing on top of a pile of rubble in the middle of a building site. The dog looked lost and forlorn, with his head raised as if he was sniffing the air. The caption beside the photo read: 'Lord, point me in the right direction.' This little prayer is relevant when we feel at a loss to know what to do, as we struggle with the cares and complexities of life and look for hope and guidance.

There was a popular song around twenty years ago with the refrain, 'Living in these troubled times.' It expresses rather well where many of us find ourselves today and where our Church finds itself at present. We are living in troubled times and it is not surprising that some people feel lost and confused. The sea of life can be rough and the winds of change can leave one floundering. The small boat is sometimes tossed about on the waves and we can feel overwhelmed by the water coming in on top of us.

Another song of more recent times comes to mind. The song is *You Raise Me Up* by Brendan Graham. He refers to those times when troubles come, when the soul is weary and the heart is burdened. At such times we are raised up so that we can stand on mountains and walk on stormy seas, filled with wonder so that we can glimpse eternity.

The image 'walk on stormy seas' reminds us of the experience of the disciples in the boat when Jesus came to them walking on the water. At first, they were terrified; they thought they were seeing a ghost. Jesus spoke to them: 'It is I, do not be afraid.' When Peter jumped out of the boat and started walking on the water to go to Jesus, he soon became aware of the wind and the waves; he took fright and felt he was sinking. He cried out to Jesus, 'Save me, Lord, I am going down.' Jesus stretched out his hand and rescued him and said to him, 'Oh man of little faith, why are you so frightened?' I always think that the question hardly needed an answer! The disciples must have felt like saying 'you know well why we are so frightened!' In another passage in the New Testament, we are told that during a storm on the lake, Jesus was asleep and when the disciples turned to him and woke him up, he challenged them for their lack of faith, and then he commanded the wind and waves, and all was calm again.

When we are troubled and frightened and turn to Jesus, we are 'pointed in the right direction'. Like Peter, we cry out to Jesus: 'Save us, help us, deliver us.' We pray that he will stretch out his arm to hold us in the palm of his hand and raise us up when we feel we are sinking. We seek and need and pray for a personal encounter with him that touches our troubled hearts, and awakens our souls and calms our fears, bringing comfort and a hopeful heart.

Jesus gives us a hope that is not deceptive:

> Today, amid so much darkness, we need to see the light of hope and to be men and women who bring hope to others. To protect every man and every woman, to look upon them with tenderness and love, is to open up a horizon of hope; it is to let a shaft of light break through the heavy clouds; it is to bring the warmth of hope! For believers, for us Christians, like Abraham, like St Joseph, the hope that we bring is set against the horizon of God, which has opened up before us in Christ. It is a hope built on the rock that is God. (Pope Francis)

To protect the whole of creation, to protect each person, especially the poorest, to protect ourselves: this is a service to which all of us are called, so that the star of hope will shine brightly. Let us protect with love all that God has given us.
(Pope Francis)

8.6. Charity, justice and true worship

A loving heart bears fruit in charity, justice and true worship. There is an unbreakable bond between these three; they belong together in a loving heart.

While charity and justice are closely related, they are not the same. The following story is often used to illustrate this:

> Once upon a time there was a town built on the banks of a large river. The river was deep and wide and had many bends in it above the place where the town was situated. One day the children of the town were playing on the bank of the river and they noticed three bodies floating in the water. They ran for help and the people quickly came and pulled the bodies out of the water. One body was dead, so they buried it. One was alive, but very ill, so they took that person to the hospital. The third was a child, so they placed the child with a family who cared for it. The same thing happened on a number of occasions. It went on for some time, until finally someone suggested that people should go up the river and see if something could be done to deal with the problems that were causing many people to end up floating in the water.

The parable highlights, in a very simple way, the difference between charity and justice. In the world of daily life, things are never that simple. I saw this for myself during my time in Africa. People who were working with the poor and sick were often the same people who were trying their best to change society and make it more just. Still the parable can be helpful to explain that charity responds to the needy and tends to them, while justice comes in when the people begin to look at the system within which we live, so as to name and change the structures that account for the fact that some people are poor and suffer so much, while others live in great luxury:

> Justice differs from charity in this way: charity is about giving a hungry person some bread, while justice is about trying to change the system, so that nobody has excess bread while some have none.[42]

Religious worship is meaningless if it does not go hand in hand with charity and justice. This is the central theme of the prophets Micah and Amos. Both of these prophets had a great passion for justice and an abhorrence of religious ritual while justice was being ignored:

> I hate, I despise your festivals, and I take no delight in your solemn assemblies. Even though you offer me your burnt offerings and grain offerings, I will not accept them; and the offerings of well-being of your fatted animals, I will not look upon. Take away from me the noise of your songs; I will not listen to the melody of your harps. But let justice roll down like waters, and righteousness like an ever-flowing stream. (Am 5:21–24)

The prophet Amos challenged the Israelites of his time about their lack of justice, their greed and their disregard for the poor:

> They sell the righteous for silver, and the needy for a pair of sandals – they who trample the head of the poor into the dust of the earth, and push the afflicted out of the way ... and in the house of their God they drink wine bought with fines they imposed. (Am 2:6–8)

For Amos and Micah, and other prophets, worship and rituals were meaningless when there was no bond with life and love and the people's hearts were far from God. True worship is the fruit of 'a loving heart' that engages in works of charity and wants justice for the poor and needy.

∞

Charity that leaves the poor in the same situation as before is not adequate. True mercy, that which God gives and teaches us, asks for justice, asks that the poor find a way out of their poverty.
(Pope Francis)

8.7. Respect and concern

A loving heart reaches out to others with respect for the dignity of each person and concern for justice and human rights in the society in which we live. We begin with a story from my youth.

The cattle fairs on the streets were very much a feature of life when I was growing up in Kerry. The farmers would arrive in the early morning with the cattle, and the 'buyers' (or 'jobbers') would appear later on. Generally, the buyers were trusted and respected, but the occasional one had a few tricks up his sleeve. The story was told about one such buyer, who had a network of 'tanglers' – local men who would tell the buyer about the farmers who were most likely to be a soft touch. The buyer could then focus his attention on these and convince them he was doing them a favour by taking the cattle off their hands. Needless to say the price paid was below the real value! The story goes that one of the tanglers was attending the Parish Mission one night and the missioner gave a powerful sermon about honesty and justice in business dealings. It left the tangler so troubled that he went to confession and told the priest about what he was up to at the fairs. When the buyer came round for the next cattle fair, the tangler was not willing to help him. Having heard his story, the buyer responded: 'The next time you go to confession, tell the priest your sins, but make sure to keep your business to yourself.'

The story highlights a talent some people have, even 'good' people, for turning a blind eye to dishonest and unjust practices in some transactions. Some areas of life are not touched and affected by the values of Christian faith, which people profess and live for the most part. Conscience can have a blind spot by seeing business as business and religion as having nothing to do with it. Notions of what is and what is not sinful can be seriously flawed, especially in this area of 'social sin' – or 'structural sin' in the more recent terminology. This can take the form of serious corruption and injustice in business, politics or indeed any area of public life. With the Celtic Tiger and its aftermath, we are aware of the immense suffering it can cause for so many people. The banks and builders, the planners and politicians have been too greedy, always seeking their own advantage, with little respect for ordinary people. A small number of people wanted wealth, even if this involved unjust and dishonest practices. Individuals can be guilty, companies can be guilty and countries can be guilty. This is social sin in various forms and it has enormous consequences. While it is bad enough here in Ireland, it is worse in Africa and other places. The level of corruption and bribery in many African countries is frightening and people who speak out pay dearly, sometimes by being brutally murdered.

Injustice and corruption are often inherent in a culture and way of life that fails to recognise social sin. And it goes on and on, unless people have a 'change of heart' that leads to respect for human rights and concern for justice. This only happens when individuals change their hearts and their ways. The call of Christ is directed to the human heart, calling each of us to change and take personal responsibility. In the last homily that he preached before he died, Archbishop Oscar Romero, the great champion of social justice, said:

> How easy it is to denounce structural injustice, institutionalised violence, social sin. All that is a reality, but where are the roots of this social sin? In the heart of every human being ... Salvation begins with the human person, with human dignity, with saving every person from sin ... this is God's call: Be converted.

When we respond to the call of Christ to be converted, we open our hearts to his love so that they can be touched and transformed. This moves us towards loving hearts that respect people's rights and show concern for justice in society – so that the rights of each person are protected, especially those of the weak and most vulnerable.

❧

Corruption is worse than any sin because it hardens the heart against feeling shame or guilt, and hearing God's call for conversion. A sinner expects forgiveness. The corrupt, on the contrary, don't, because they don't feel they have sinned. One who is corrupt is so holed up in the satisfaction of his own self-sufficiency that his bloated self-esteem refuses to face the reality of his fraudulent and opportunistic behaviour.
(Pope Francis)

CHAPTER NINE

Seasons of the Heart

*How long will your hearts be closed, will you
love what is futile and seek what is false.*
(Ps 4)

*Take delight in the Lord and he will give you
the desires of your heart.*
(Ps 37:4)

9.1. Healing a wounded, wintry heart

We begin our 'Seasons of the Heart' with the wintry conditions that one experiences when the heart is wounded and there is no healing and it ends up closed, dark and cold unless it is touched and transformed by love.

The Irish novelist, the late John McGahern, won an award for his book *Amongst Women*. It deals with lack of love in family life and the devastating consequences of this for all involved. The father is too hurt and too damaged to love: his heart is closed and he cannot provide love for his children because he himself has not known it in his own life. The Moran family prayed the rosary every night and went to Mass on Sundays, but this made very little difference to their lives, as religion and life stayed strangers to each other. Here were people who needed to be rescued from hurt and anger, and who found little comfort in their faith, which was not so much a search for truth and love as adherence to a set of religious practices that had to be conformed to in the community.

Old Moran was hardened by the life he had experienced, and there was no escaping his anger and aggression. Even when he dies there is no peace for the family, as they search the past, looking in vain for love and acceptance. His heart was wintry and cold, frozen over with a layer of bitterness. And that cycle repeats itself. Unless their hearts are healed, children are likely to starve their own children of what they themselves have never known. The past and the future are linked in the chain of love or the lack of it. The wintry, wounded heart can only be healed through an experience of being loved and accepted.

It is a great blessing to love and be loved – to know somebody loves us, listens to us, understands us and really accepts us. It may be a father or a mother, a husband or a wife, a brother or a sister, or a close friend. St Augustine described a friend as 'someone who knows all about you and still loves and accepts you'. And he also wrote that 'the love with which we love each other is the same love that comes from God'. We are caught up in the to-and-fro of the love of God in our ordinary human relationships. We are channels of God's love and acceptance to each other. St Paul puts it like this:

> Blessed be the God and Father of our Lord Jesus Christ, the Father
> of mercies and the God of all consolation, who consoles us in all
> our affliction, so that we may be able to console those who are in
> any affliction with the consolation with which we ourselves are
> consoled by God. (2 Cor 1:3–5)

This is the kind of consolation and comfort that thaws out a
closed, wounded, wintry heart and opens it up to new life.

Perhaps we can pause for a moment to reflect on the season
of winter as it affects our own hearts and how we find comfort
and consolation that helps us to be more loving and open.

A final observation: Institutions, including the institutional
Church, can exhibit cold, frozen hearts. While recognising the
great good that the Church does for so many people in all walks
of life, we also know that some individuals and groups find the
response of the Church to their plight cold and heartless. In recent
times, Pope Francis is moving towards more tolerance and
inclusion:

> The Church has sometimes locked itself into small things, in small
> minded rules. The Church is a home for all, not a small chapel
> that can only hold a small group of selected people … I dream of
> a Church that is a mother and shepherdess. The ministers of the
> Church must be ministers of mercy, accompanying people like
> the Good Samaritan, who washes and cleans the wounds of the
> man he found on the road.

⁙

In every man and in every woman there is a wound, inflicted by failures,
humiliations, bad conscience. Perhaps it was caused at a time when we needed
infinite understanding and acceptance, and nobody was there to give it …
Transfigured by Christ, it is changed into a focus of energy … where
communion, friendship and understanding burst forth.
(Brother Roger of Taize)

9.2. Awareness of our 'secret sins'

When jealousy and resentment invade the heart in a serious way, they bring cold, icy, wintry conditions with them – a hard place to be while one waits for a thaw that can lead to a better place. Jealousy and resentment can be very destructive to one's relationships with others and also damaging for oneself. Here is a story from the East to illustrate this:

> There were two neighbours who were very good friends. God appeared to one of them in a dream and told him he would give him anything he asked for on condition that his neighbour could have twice as much. The man decided to give it a try. He asked for five acres of land ... and he got them; his neighbour got ten acres. He asked for a well ... and he got it; his neighbour got two wells. And so the story went on. Everything the man asked for he got, but his neighbour got twice as much and, of course, was much better off.
>
> Needless to say, the friendship suffered. The man began to feel jealous of his neighbour and gradually bitterness crept into his heart. He resented his neighbour's good fortune. Finally, he could take it no longer so he decided he would have to change his tactics. As he wondered how he would be able to get at the neighbour, one day he came up with an idea. He asked to go blind in one eye – which he did. And, the neighbour went blind in both eyes. The man got satisfaction out of this and he got pleasure out of watching his neighbour pottering around his house with a stick, having to take great care to avoid falling into one of the two wells that God gave him. Then one-day disaster struck; the man who had the dream was so busy watching the blind neighbour that he stumbled and fell into his own well and was drowned.

This story is used as a parable to impress on people that feelings of resentment and jealousy, revenge, anger and bitterness, are destructive not only for others but also for oneself. This is clearly expressed in the saying 'Resentment is like drinking poison and hoping it will kill your enemies.' Feelings of anger and resentment can be terribly destructive if we linger on them and nurse them along from day to day. These negative, destructive feelings can fester in our hearts. It is a slippery slope, as the man in the story discovered. It can start off innocently enough, but inevitably one thing leads to another and eventually friendship is weakened, eroded and even destroyed. Sometimes it is frightening to see how quickly this can happen when the human heart becomes resentful; people who were friends may end up no longer talking to each other. Positions become entrenched, attitudes harden and the heart is closed, as pride creeps in and anger freezes into resentment. All this is destructive for everybody involved. It can happen between friends, neighbours and even members of a family.

In one of his sermons, Blessed John Henry Newman spoke about 'our secret sins' – feelings of envy, jealousy, revenge, bitterness and resentment – the same destructive feelings that were mentioned in the story. These are our 'secret sins'. Many may not know about them, apart from ourselves and a few others who are affected or involved. These are the hidden, silent, secret sins that can be deeply rooted in a cold, wintry heart.

Cardinal Newman also wrote about the need to have an abiding sorrow for these 'secret sins'. This involves an awareness of our 'secret sins' – the inner feelings of resentment and jealousy – and a humble desire to be rid of them through the loving mercy of God. With an experience of the warmth of God's love and mercy that comes to us through Jesus, a resentful heart can change and become mellow and warm.

⌘

I found Jesus closer to me than I am to myself. How can I perceive his presence within me? It is full of life and efficacy, and no sooner has he entered than my sluggish soul is awakened. He moves and warms and wounds my heart, hard and stony and sick though it be.
(St Bernard of Clairvaux)

9.3. A change of heart

'If winter comes can spring be far behind?', the saying goes. And spring brings change and growth, light and new life. This can happen with a human heart that has been cold and frozen. Spring arrives when the heart is touched in a deep way and awakened to God's abiding presence and love. When the seed of God's love is sown and takes root and blossoms, it brings repentance, conversion, a change of heart.

We turn to St Augustine here. He tells the story of his 'change of heart' (conversion) in his *Confessions*.[43] It happened in AD 386, when he was thirty-two years old, and deeply troubled in mind, heart and spirit. He describes what happened when relief finally came: 'It was as if before a soft peaceful light streaming into my heart, all the dark shadows of doubt fled away.'

Augustine thought that he was searching for God all his life but found, through his conversion experience, that God was always present with him, searching for him and calling on him. This comes out clearly in this famous passage, often quoted:

> Too late have I loved you, O beauty so ancient and so new ... you were within me, while I was outside: it was there that I sought you ... You were with me but I was not with you ... You have called to me and cried out, and you have shattered my deafness ... you have put my blindness to flight! ... I have tasted you and hunger and thirst after you. You have touched me and I have burnt for your peace.

These are powerful images expressing Augustine's sense of God trying to get through to him. It is good to reflect on each image – notice that the senses are involved: hearing, seeing, tasting and touching. He woke up to God's presence within him and all around him, and realised that the experience of God's love in his heart was the driving force throughout his journey to God. He concluded that it is not fear or guilt but love that motivates a person and brings about a change of heart. And he was sure that God's love is within: 'Wherever you are, wherever you may be praying, he who hears you is within you, hidden within.'

Augustine was well aware of the struggle involved in living out the change of heart in daily life. He knew that a 'change of heart' does not come easily; it involved an inner struggle that lasted a lifetime. Though his conversion had its dramatic moments, he did not regard it as a once-and-for-all experience; it was a slow maturing process of a lifetime. All through life, he felt he was a sinner before a God of love, mercy and compassion. He was on a pilgrimage to God, always on the move, going deeper into the mystery. He was convinced of God's search for the sinner and of our need to discover this for ourselves, so that we can experience God's love in our hearts – an experience that leads to change, growth and new life – an experience of springtime in the heart. This process is greatly aided by prayer, which, as we saw in an earlier reflection, is the human heart's desire for God being lived out in daily life.

For Augustine, the human heart is restless until it rests in God. We have to stop struggling against the current and let go, allowing the Spirit of God to guide us. Then and only then is the heart really changed, awakened and transformed. His conversion in AD 386 was the beginning of such an experience for him. It was a personal encounter of the heart with Christ. He concluded that it was part of God's plan that he should first experience his own weakness, restlessness and need for Christ on his journey 'into the blessedness, which we are not only meant to know, but also to dwell in'.

∽

You have made us for yourself, O Lord, and our hearts are restless, until they rest in thee.
(St Augustine)

It is always springtime in the heart that loves God.
(St John Vianney)

9.4. A compassionate heart

There is consoling warmth about compassion. It crosses all boundaries of class and creed. It belongs to all groups of people and is the private property of none. A compassionate heart is filled with the warmth, light and life of summer; it is alive, committed and involved with others in their suffering.

When I was a student in Mill Hill London many years ago, a famous scripture scholar came to give us a special lecture. He began by asking the question: 'What texts of scripture give us the basic teaching of Jesus?' We came up with various texts about the kingdom of God, repentance, the Beatitudes, and the great commandment to love God, self and others. His response was positive, but he went on to say that he would like to add another text that contained the invitation to 'be compassionate, just as your father is compassionate' (Lk 6:36, NLT). He said that for him this text contained the core of the teaching of Jesus. It covers everything that is required of us as followers of Christ.

Over the years, I have come to appreciate what the scripture professor was saying. Compassion is a wonderful divine and human gift that is found in a compassionate heart. It is what we experience when somebody comes to our help in times of trouble and great suffering. We all have such times on our journey through life. It can be the loss of a loved one and the sense of grief and pain that we experience or it can be suffering that comes with serious illness. At such times there is often a great outpouring of friendship and support from family members, friends and neighbours. This is especially true when it is a sudden death of a younger person through illness or a tragic accident or, worse still, through suicide. In these situations, people are greatly helped by the tremendous outpouring of love and compassion from family, friends and neighbours. Such tragedies bring out the best in people. You can see love and compassion in action, at the deepest level.

Compassion means to suffer with or to enter into the suffering of another person and journey with them through the suffering. It is the love that we are capable of because God's love has been poured into our hearts; it is a love that is willing to give, to sacrifice and to suffer with another person. This is what we mean when we talk about love as 'compassion' and 'a compassionate heart'.

Compassion can sometimes take us into dark places of anguish and suffering in other peoples' lives. With faith and love, we feel our way into the great sea of human pain that surrounds us. So much suffering is borne in silence and in secret. Many people who suffer are unable to reveal the depths of anguish and pain that they endure. Others have to make their painful pilgrimage very much in the public eye and even before the glare of television cameras, as was the case with Gerry and Kate McCann, after the disappearance of their daughter Madeleine in May 2007. Their every move was covered. But so too was the great outpouring of support and compassion that they experienced. I am sure that they were together as mother and father in the dark abyss of their suffering and in a sense they were two people very much alone there, but many people tried to reach out to them with great compassion.

Love as compassion is the love revealed in Christ. He suffered and died for us out of love: 'greater love than this no one has than to lay down his life for his friends'. We are called to imitate Christ's compassion, which has the warmth, light and life of summer about it. We need to be compassionate towards ourselves as well as others. Silent prayer is one of the practices that can help us to become more compassionate.

❧

Christ's gaze purifies our hearts; the light of his countenance illumines the eyes of our hearts and teaches us to see everything in the light of his truth and his compassion for all people.
(CCC 2715)

9.5. A joyful heart – the warmth of summer

In the film, *The Bucket List*, Jack Nicholson and Morgan Freeman, who are both dying of cancer, agree that two questions will be asked of them when they pass beyond the gates of death: 'Did you find joy in life and did you bring joy to others?'

I think of these questions in relation to Peter whom I got to know when I lived in Kisumu Town in western Kenya. He suffers from a severe physical disability, having been born with his lower body and both legs seriously deformed. He is small in stature, gifted with his hands, bright and cheerful. He ran a 'small business' (as he called it) under an acacia tree in front of the Sunset Hotel, not far from our Mill Hill House. I met him most days during my years in Kisumu. He sold little items to tourists visiting the hotel. At his station under the tree, he sat on a small stool and when there were no customers or visitors at his little stall, he was busy working with banana fibres and other materials making birds, beads, ear-rings, necklaces and so on.

Early one morning Peter arrived at our Mill Hill House in great distress. I knew there had to be some terrible tragedy, as I had never seen him upset about anything. The tears streamed down his cheeks as he told me that his young brother had been killed in an accident near his home, which was fifty miles from Kisumu. He was distraught. He needed money to travel home and to buy a coffin. He would also have to pay for food for the funeral, as he was the only family member earning any money. My heart went out to him. I gave him the money he needed and prayed for him and his family as he rode off on his bicycle. I felt very sorry for him, thinking of what lay ahead of him.

A couple of weeks later, Peter was back at his station under the acacia tree. He looked sad but said he was relieved to be back. He told me that he would soon have money for me. True to his word, he arrived to me the following week with some of the money. This would rarely happen with those who borrow! I was impressed with his honesty and told him to hold on to the money. I continued to see him in the weeks that followed and soon his smile was back.

Peter found joy in life, despite the heavy cross of personal disability that was his lot from birth. His face radiated with a wonderful smile that came from a joyful heart. He was grateful too, often thanking God for what he was able to do. He had good reason to be bitter and resentful with the hand that life had dealt him but he managed to cope with his disability remarkably well. We meet people like him in many walks of life who bring joy to others – perhaps sometimes without knowing it.

Joy and gratitude are closely related. They flow from a heart that receives and gives in the to-and-fro of love.

I will finish here with a little story:

> The Spirit once led Saint Anthony of the Desert to the home of a physician where he told Anthony he would show him his equal. Anthony asked the physician, 'What do you do?' And the physician replied, 'I heal those who come to me. More than I need I do not take. More than I can use, I give to the poor, and all day I sing the Sanctus in my heart.' (Joan Chittister, *The Breath of the Soul*)

The physician's 'Sanctus' expressing his praise and thanks to God came from a joyful heart that was aware of God's love. In his work as a physician, he lived that love and shared it with all who came to him. In doing this, he found joy in life and brought joy to others – as Peter did and so many others do. While such people have ups and downs in life like everyone else, most of the time they manage to live in a 'season of the heart' that brings the warmth of summer to those they meet on life's journey.

꧁꧂

Like the joy of the sea coming home to shore, may the music of laughter break through your soul.
(John O'Donohue, *Benedictus*)

Trust in God and follow Jesus faithfully, and you will be witnesses of the joy that flows from intimate union with him.
(Pope Benedict XVI)

9.6. A mature, mellow heart

Autumn is the 'Season of mists and mellow fruitfulness, close bosom friend of the maturing sun' (John Keats). The human heart has an autumn season when it becomes mature and mellow. This begins to happen when a loving heart bears fruit in prayer, love and justice. We find these three linked together in this text from the Prophet Micah: 'This is what the Lord your God asks of you: to act justly, to love tenderly, and to walk humbly with God' (Micah 6:8). Years ago, I wrote an article in *Saint Joseph's Advocate*, in which I quoted this text. Some time later I got a letter from one of our readers, an elderly man, who thanked me for drawing his attention to such a wonderful verse of scripture. He felt that it contains the best advice that any parent or teacher could offer to the young generation.

Micah 6:8 is a summary of the message of three of the great prophets. We find Amos's call for justice, Hosea's appeal for steadfast love that binds people to God and to one another, and Isaiah's plea for the quiet prayer and faith of the humble who walk with God. Here we have prayer, love and justice, which belong together in an unbreakable bond. Prayer is never just a private, personal, isolated activity. It is always related to love in the interpersonal area and to justice in the public area. Love is the fruit of faith and prayer. Justice flows from love that is concerned for the rights and dignity of each person.

In the life we live, it is important to try to integrate prayer, love and justice – into personal, interpersonal and public areas. It is easy to fall into a kind of personal piety that has little effect on relationships with others and on our place in society. It is also possible to devote much time to our own 'inner work' and stop there, leaving God and others out of it. It can also happen that people become preoccupied with social justice issues and the environment while losing sight of the need for prayer and charity. Christian spirituality allows for a particular interest and emphasis in one of the three areas, but the other two cannot be neglected. A genuine spirituality has to be grounded in the spiritual, concerned for the well-being of others, and committed to building a more just society where all can live.

The late Cardinal Suenens and the late Archbishop Helder Camera were well aware of the need to integrate prayer, love and justice. The cardinal was involved in the 'charismatic movement', which was sometimes criticised for a lack of social involvement. On the other hand, the archbishop was involved in the struggle for liberation in South America, which was sometimes criticised for being weak on the spiritual dimension – though he himself would certainly be exempt from such criticism; he prayed for two hours in the early hours of every morning. These two great men got together and wrote a book entitled: *Charismatic Renewal and Social Action – a Dialogue*.[44] The two authors brought their personal experience to the exposition of the theme that Christians are committed prayerfully to God and lovingly to one another, while they are also committed socially to the building up of God's kingdom in the societies in which they live. Here we find the three areas integrated: personal prayer, love in interpersonal relationships and a commitment to justice for all.

We can express this in the language of the heart. When our hearts are being touched and transformed by the love of God, we begin to walk with a humble heart before God, to live with a loving heart that goes out to others in tender love, and to respond with a compassionate heart to the need for justice in today's world. When this starts happening we are moving into the autumn season, towards a heart that is humble, loving, mature, mellow and fruitful.

⤜⤛

Gustavo Gutiérrez, the father of liberation theology, suggests that, to have a healthy spirituality, we must feed our souls in three ways: through prayer, both private and communal; through the practice of justice; and through having those things in our lives (good friendships, wine-drinking, creativity, and healthy leisure) that help keep the soul mellow and grateful.[45]

9.7. A grateful heart

When the human heart experiences an autumn season, there can be a certain melancholy or nostalgia about it, but feelings of gratitude and forgiveness are also part of this season of the heart.

To mark his seventy-fifth birthday, the novelist Morris West published a book of reflections, entitled *A View from the Ridge*, in which he suggests that, at the age of seventy-five, 'gratitude' is one word that you need to have in your spiritual vocabulary. As he sees it, when you reach a certain age, gratitude begins to drown out and cure the hurts in your life. He feels that life has served him, as it serves everyone, sometimes well and sometimes ill, but he has learned to be grateful for the gifts of life, especially for the love with which he has been richly endowed during his life.

Gratitude comes with feelings that run deep within the affective experiential side of life. It is closely related to joy and it aids in having sensitivity to the needs of others, especially in their suffering. Gratitude is also the heart of prayer. It connects us in a wonderful way with God and grows out of our experience of God's love in our lives. We can be grateful for what we have or we can be resentful of others. We can look back in anger or we can look back with a grateful heart. Gratitude and forgiveness belong together:

> The fruit of gratitude and maturity is forgiveness. Just as smoke follows fire, forgiveness follows gratitude. Gratitude ultimately supports and fuels all genuine virtue; it is the real basis of holiness and the source of love itself. And its major fruit is forgiveness. When we are grateful we more easily find the strength to forgive.[46]

But reaching forgiveness can be a real struggle, as we saw in the sad figure of the older brother of the prodigal son who lacked forgiveness. He resented the welcome that was given to his brother. He had stayed at home doing the work and being good and doing everything right. He could not forgive his prodigal brother or even his father, though his father is patient with him and treats him graciously. His heart had cold bitter spots that needed the warmth of forgiveness and healing. Perhaps he came to that – the story does not tell us how it went.

Ronald Rolheiser wrote about Andrew Greeley's review of Frank McCourt's book, *Angela's Ashes*. Andrew praised McCourt for being a brilliant writer, but challenged him for being unforgiving with words to this effect:

> Granted, your life has been unfair. Your father was an alcoholic, your mother didn't protect you from the effects of that, you grew up in dire poverty, and you suffered a series of mini-injustices under the Irish social services, the Irish Church, the Irish educational system, and the Irish weather! So, let me give you some advice: before you die, forgive! Forgive your father for being an alcoholic, forgive your mother for not protecting you, forgive the Church for whatever ways it failed you, forgive Ireland for the poverty, rain, and bad teachers it inflicted on you, forgive yourself for the failures of your own life, and then forgive God because life isn't fair. Just forgive so that you don't die an angry and bitter man.[47]

These words are so true and so challenging. What Frank McCourt needed, and indeed what we all need, is to reach the stage of being grateful so that 'gratitude begins to drown out and cure the hurts in our life' – as Morris West suggests. When we can look back with a grateful heart we have reached a stage of being able to forgive people for the hurts inflicted on us. Most of us have been wounded along the way. No one sails through life with his or her heart totally healthy and whole. It is often a struggle to bring warmth and forgiveness to the cold bitter spots that are left by life's hurts. We cannot manage it on our own – nor do we have to. We are invited to trust in the abiding presence of a loving God who comes to us with healing and help, with mercy and forgiveness: 'God hovers in love over the fragments of our brokenness; over the dark and storm-tossed waters, God hovers in mercy' (St Augustine). This is surely something for which we can be truly grateful.

❦

If the only prayer you can say in your life is 'thank you', that would suffice.
(Meister Eckhart)

Appendix

Simple Forms of Meditation

To help quieten the mind, calm the soul,
and open the heart to God's abiding presence.

Simple forms of meditation

As this book of reflections took shape I had mixed feelings about including an appendix on forms of meditation. It was there in an earlier draft and later I decided to remove it but it found its way back in with encouragement from Noel Keating who read the reflections and felt that information on meditation would complement them.

Noel is involved with Christian Meditation Ireland and he feels there is a great need for guidance with meditation as he sees the difference it makes to personal prayer. It helps those who want to go deeper and encounter God's presence at a personal, experiential level. Noel is presently the national coordinator of a very interesting pilot project to promote Christian meditation with children in schools.[48]

On a personal note, I am often surprised at the way a form of meditation can help quieten the mind, calm the soul and awaken the heart to an awareness of God. I can see why spiritual writers encourage us to develop a prayerful practice using one of the simple methods of meditation that are readily available to us. Prayer is always God's gift, but we can do something to be prepared, ready, awake and open to God's loving presence, touching and transforming our hearts and lives.[49]

Since the word 'heart' keeps coming up, we need to recall what was written about it in the introduction. With a quotation from the *New Dictionary of Catholic Spirituality*, we saw that the word 'heart' when it is used in the Bible and in Christian writings means far more than it does in ordinary English. It symbolises the entire inner life, inner being of the person, involving the soul, memory, mind and spirit. It is home to human experience, feelings and emotions that are so much part of the inner life but also involve and affect the body. Our thoughts, words and actions flow from the heart. This is the context in which we talk about meditation/contemplation opening the heart to God.

Opening the heart to God

In the reflections we explored the core theme that the eternal God is ever-present with us in the lives we live. We are more likely to be aware of this if we have grown up in a family where we experienced love. Our hearts will have been touched and awakened by the experience of love in a way that opens them to God. If this happened, our awareness of God's abiding presence has been there from the beginning as true knowledge of the heart that can stay with us throughout our lives.

While this is true, more of us, as we grow into adulthood, need to make our own that which we have taken for granted through childhood and begun to question in adolescence. When we leave home and begin to make a life for ourselves, the demands of daily living can sometimes drown out the inner voice and the earlier experience. But where the awareness of love was strong in childhood, there will be occasions in adult life when it doesn't take much to touch the heart and re-awaken it to knowledge of the eternal God who is ever-present with us.

For those whose childhood was far from idyllic, it may take something more to awaken the heart to an awareness of God's closeness. Richard Rohr writes that great love and great suffering are the two main pathways that bring us to that awareness. It is easy to see how it happens when we travel the pathway of love, but the pathway of suffering is another matter. Some of us grow resentful and bitter when a heavy cross comes our way, while others live with an awareness that God is always near us and with us in the trials and troubles of life.

It is the work of a lifetime to go deeper and deeper into the mystery of God. Jesus and the Holy Spirit are at the centre of the journey. St Paul's beautiful prayer makes this clear:

> I pray that, according to the riches of his glory, he may grant that you may be strengthened in your inner being with power through his Spirit, and that Christ may dwell in your hearts through faith, as you are being rooted and grounded in love. I pray that you may have the power to comprehend, with all the saints, what is the breadth and length and height and depth, and to know the love of Christ that surpasses knowledge, so that you may be filled with all the fullness of God … who by the power at work within us is able to accomplish abundantly far more than all we can ask or imagine … (Eph: 3:16–21)

As long as we remember the place of Christ and the role of the Holy Spirit, the reflections and the use of forms of meditation can help us on our way into the mystery by stirring our restless hearts to yearn for a closer relationship with the loving God who embraces us.

The prayer of the heart

In the introduction, I began with the story about Joshua Bell playing his violin at a Washington metro station. Over a thousand people passed and just a single person recognised one of the finest classical musicians in the world playing some of the best music ever written on one of the most expensive instruments ever made.

We were left to ponder the need to be more reflective and more in tune with the deeper aspects of the lives we live so that we can become more aware of the mystery of God with us and within us. This is where prayer (meditation, contemplation) comes in and can be a great help. Commitment to a regular period of personal, silent prayer each day is one of the best ways to open our hearts to God. Such prayer is called 'the prayer of the heart' – it can lead us, with the Spirit's help, into heart-knowledge, experiential knowledge of God's abiding presence.

Many of us were brought up with the description of prayer in the catechism, as the raising of the mind and heart to God. Unfortunately, in teaching people how to pray, the Church has tended to emphasise mental and vocal prayer over the prayer of the heart. All three are important, but we will never come to heart-knowledge through the mind and words alone. To get to such knowledge we need 'the prayer of the heart' (meditation or contemplation).

The prayer of the heart is the kind of prayer that engages a person's whole being, touching one at the level of experience, feelings and emotions. It engages the heart in a way that leads to intimate, personal, experiential knowledge of God's loving presence with us in Christ and the Holy Spirit. With such an experience we cannot but be changed and transformed into better human beings through following Christ more closely with lives of prayer, love and service.

Note: Some people find that dovetailing the day with prayer works well – praying in the morning and the evening. In one of the reflections I referred to the Irish practice of covering the hot embers with ashes last thing at night and of stirring the *griosach* (the hot embers in the ashes) first thing in the morning. Not a bad image for daily prayer!

> *May the Lord direct your hearts towards the love of God and to the steadfastness of Christ.*
> (2 Thess 3:5)

Three forms of meditation using a 'mantra'

We need to be aware that these forms of meditation are actually forms of contemplation. Although often used today as stand-alone methods, they were originally seen as the final stage in the process of praying scripture with the heart, a method of prayer known as *Lectio Divina* (divine reading). We also note that from earliest times, contemplation was regarded as the normal development of a Christian prayer life.

Ideally, those who use these methods of meditation will also incorporate reflection on scripture and other forms of prayer into their regular prayer practice. Some people find *Lectio Divina* or Gospel contemplation helpful ways to pray with scripture. And of course the rosary remains popular with people of a certain age group. The rosary combines vocal prayer with meditation; while addressing the words to Mary, one reflects on the mysteries.

In each of the three methods of meditation that we are considering here, a person is encouraged to use a 'prayer-word' or 'mantra', which can be a single word or a phrase. It may be a word from scripture or one that arises spontaneously from within your heart, such as the word 'Abba', or the name 'Jesus', or the word 'Maranatha', or it may be a phrase such as 'Jesus, Son of God. Have mercy on me.'

The 'mantra' is repeated slowly, silently within oneself, perhaps in harmony with one's breathing. This helps us to go beyond thoughts, beyond the senses and the rational mind to the heart where the Spirit of God is present.

A very simple form of prayer without words or images, contemplation (or meditation as the word is used here) opens our hearts to God dwelling within us. In this type of prayer we spiral down into the deepest centre of ourselves to the point of silence and stillness within us where we experience God's presence most intimately and become aware that we are being held in God's embrace. In using these forms of prayer, one simply sits in silence in God's presence seeking to quieten the mind, calm the soul and awaken the heart to an awareness of God.

(a) Christian meditation

John Main OSB, writes that 'the Spirit of God dwells in our hearts in silence' and recommends the word 'Maranatha' as a prayer word or mantra. 'Maranatha' is an Aramaic word, the language that Jesus spoke. He regards it as probably the most ancient prayer in the Church. It is the last verse in both first Corinthians and the Book of Revelation. It is translated as 'Come Lord Jesus, Come.'

John Main stresses that St Benedict drew attention to this method of prayer as far back as the sixth century, when he directed his monks to read the conferences of John Cassian.[50] Cassian recommended that anyone who wanted to learn to pray continually should take a single short verse and repeat this verse over and over again.

Method:
1. *Say the word gently and in a relaxed way – 'Ma-ra-na-tha' – repeating each syllable slowly in harmony with your breathing.*
2. *Listen to the word as you say it and try not to think of anything while you meditate.*
3. *If thoughts come, acknowledge them, but do not entertain them during the period of meditation.*
4. *Meditate each morning and evening for between twenty and thirty minutes.*

[Louis Hughes mentions that he uses the word 'Iosa' (the Irish word for

'Jesus') and allows the (silent) 'ee' sound to match the intake of breath and the 'sa' sound to match the out-breath.][51]

(b) Centering prayer

Another method of meditation using a 'mantra' is called 'centering prayer'. Two Cistercian monks, Basil Pennington and Thomas Keating, have promoted this approach. They have written extensively about it. They stress that it comes from the Christian tradition, especially from *The Cloud of Unknowing*, which was written by an unknown English Catholic in the fourteenth century.

Basil Pennington comments on 'centering prayer' that we can 'see how pure this prayer is. In active forms of prayer, we use thoughts and images as sacraments for reaching out to God. In this form of prayer, we go beyond them; we leave them behind, as we go to God himself abiding in our depths'.[52]

Method:
There are three simple steps proposed by Basil Pennington:

1. *At the beginning of prayer take a minute or two to quiet down and then move in faith to God dwelling in our depths; at the end of the prayer take several minutes to come out, mentally praying the 'Our Father' or some other prayer.*
2. *After resting for some time in the centre of faith-filled love, take up a single, simple word that expresses your response and begin to let it repeat itself within.*
3. *Whenever in the course of the prayer you become aware of anything else, simply return to the prayer word.*

(c) The Jesus prayer

'The Jesus prayer' is another method of meditation using a 'mantra'. This ancient prayer comes to us from the Eastern Orthodox Churches and links us with believers of the earliest New Testament days. The exercise of this prayer is to silently pray it, continuously and quietly; we can let it coincide with our breathing. It becomes a 'mantra' along the lines that we have described earlier.

Method:

1. *Sit down alone and in silence. Lower your head, shut your eyes and breathe out gently; imagine yourself looking into your own heart. Carry your mind, i.e. your thoughts, from your head to your heart.*
2. *In harmony with your breathing say: 'Lord Jesus Christ have mercy on me.' Say it moving your lips gently or simply say it in your mind. Try to put all other thoughts aside. Be calm, be patient and repeat the process very frequently.*[53]

Comment on thoughts and distractions:

As regards thoughts and distractions that arise during meditation, John Main points out that they come spontaneously and we cannot prevent them arising – but we can choose not to entertain them while we meditate. What we are called to do in meditation, which is a state of relaxed alertness, is to acknowledge the thoughts that arise and let them go for the time being, and return to our mantra with loving kindness towards ourselves.

In the silence of meditation it may well occur that important issues in our lives that need to be resolved come to the surface and it may be essential that we return to them later and take steps to deal appropriately with them. Sometimes meditation can be quite frustrating as we are bombarded over and over again by wave after wave of thoughts but it is an important part of the discipline that we acknowledge each one and then gently but firmly set it aside and bring our attention back to our 'prayer-word' or mantra. Every time we do this, we return to God and renew our intention to sit quietly in God's presence.

In doing so, we leave ourselves open to the Spirit; we allow ourselves to become Christ-centred rather than centred on ourselves. Our faith tells us that deep within the recesses of our heart, deep in the silence, something profound is taking place and we are being transformed at a level of consciousness that is beyond our awareness. It is the kind of knowing beyond knowledge that St Paul refers to in the letter to the Ephesians (Eph 3:14–20). St Ignatius tells us that the touch of God is light and gentle, like a drop of water on a sponge. We need to be very still to get a real sense of that gentle touch which transforms us. Meditation helps us to be still.

Notes

1.   This is the message of St John of the Cross, as Jean Vanier sees it. See his foreword to *The impact of God* by Iain Matthew, Hodder and Stoughton, London, 1995.
2.   Gene Weingarten, 'Pearls before Breakfast', *The Washington Post*, 8 April 2007.
3.   St Augustine, *Sermon 38 on the New Testament*, n.5.
4.   *Catechism of the Catholic Church*, n.2710.
5.   St John of the Cross, *The Spiritual Canticle*, 35.1. and 29.3.
6.   Ronald Rolheiser, 'Dark Memory', *The Catholic Herald*, 12 November 2006.
7.   St John of the Cross, *The Spiritual Canticle*, 14.
8.   Jean Vanier, *The Broken Body*, Darton, Longman and Todd, 1988, p. 138, 140. Jean Vanier is the founder of L'Arche, an international federation of group homes for people with developmental disabilities and those who assist them.
9.   Here I am indebted to Ronald Rolheiser's frequent writings about this – such as 'Born into the Ordinary' in *The Catholic Herald*, 29 December 1989.
10. For more see Ronald Rolheiser 'Domestic and Monastic', *The Irish Catholic*, 31 January 2008.
11. Brian Keenan, *An Evil Cradling*, Vintage Books, 1992, p. 99.
12. Henri J. M. Nouwen, *The Return of the Prodigal Son*, DLT, London 1994, p. 8.
13. Robert L. Moore, *Facing the Dragon – Confronting personal and Spiritual grandiosity*, Chiron Publications, Wilmette, Illinois, 2003, p. 1 (There is more about Robert Moore in reflection 6.3.).
14. *Catechism of the Catholic Church*, n.2710.
15. In this reflection, I must acknowledge my indebtedness to Daniel O'Leary's article, 'Breeze that blows open the heart', in his book, *Already Within*, published by Columba Press, 2007, p. 141.
16. Catherine de Hueck Doherty (Servant of God), *Re-Entry into Faith: 'Courage, be not afraid'*, Madonna House Publications, Combermere, Ontario, 2012.
17. John Moriarty, *Serious Sounds*, Lilliput Press, Dublin, 2007, p. 62.
18. Ibid, p. 62, 63.

19 John Moriarty, *Nostos*, Lilliput Press, Dublin, 2001, p. 491.
20 Fr Anthony Bellagamba has written an interesting article about these traditions in: *Towards African Christian Maturity*, Chiea Extension Programme, 1987, p. 101ff.
21 Daniel J. O'Leary, *Travelling Light*, Columba Press, Dublin, 2001, p. 200.
22 Henri Nouwen, *The Return of the Prodigal Son*, DLT, 1992, p. 106.
23 Ronald Rolheiser, 'What Does One Say', *The Irish Catholic*, 3 November 2007.
24 *The Confessions of Saint Augustine*, trans. John K. Ryan, Image Books, 1960, Book VIII, chs 8–12, and Book X, ch. 27.
25 *Michelangelo: The Poems*, trans. C. Ryan, J. M. Dent, 1996.
26 Cardinal Timothy Dolan, *Priests for the Third Millennium*, Our Sunday Visitor, 2000.
27 Mass was celebrated on these 'Mass Rocks' in penal times. They were in remote places.
28 Pope Benedict, *God is Love*, p. 33, 38
29 *Catechism of the Catholic Church*, n.2715.
30 *Redemptoris Missio*, nos 28 and 29.
31 From the Irish word *grios* or *griosach* meaning 'hot embers in ashes' or 'glowing'.
32 Fergal Keane, *All of these People*, Harper Perennial, 2006, p. 5, and in the P.S., at the end of the book.
33 Ronald Rolheiser, 'God's Voice as Invitation', *The Catholic Herald*, 29 April 2007.
34 Michael Paul Gallagher, *Free To Believe*, A Campion book, 1987, ch. 1.
35 Piet van Breemen, *As Bread that is Broken*, Dimension Books, Denville, New Jersey, p. 9.
36 Robert L. Moore, *Facing the Dragon – Confronting personal and Spiritual grandiosity*, Chiron Publications, Wilmette, Illinois, 2003. The quotations that follow below are from p. 191 and p. 182.
37 Frank O'Connor, *Traveller's Samples (A book of Short Stories)*, London: Macmillan, 1951. New York: Knopf, 1951.
38 Jules J. Toner, *Discernment of Spirits*, Institute of Jesuit Resources, 1982, p. 22.
39 You can read the full story in *Can I Give Him My Eyes?* by Richard Moore with Don Mullan, published by Hachette Books, 2009.
40 Fr Wilfrid Harrington OP, stressed this in lectures that I attended some years ago.
41 Daniel J. O'Leary, *Traveling Light*, Columba Press, 2001, Dublin, p. 103.
42 Ronald Rolheiser, *Seeking Spirituality*, Hodder and Stoughton, London, 1998, p. 160.
43 *The Confessions of Saint Augustine*, translated by John K. Ryan, Image

Books, 1960, Book VIII, chs 8–12, and Book X, ch. 27.

44 Cardinal Suenens and Archbishop Camera, *Charismatic Renewal and Social Action: A Dialogue*, Malines Doc. 3, DLT, London 1980.

45 Ronald Rolheiser, *Seeking Spirituality*, Hodder and Stoughton, London, 1998, p. 64.

46 Ronald Rolheiser, 'Simplifying our Spiritual Vocabulary', *The Irish Catholic*, 29 May 2011.

47 Ibid.

48 You can get more information on this project on the website: www.christianmeditation.ie, and also in the article 'Christian Meditation with Children', by Noel Keating, *Intercom*, October 2013, p. 29. I want also to acknowledge my indebtedness to Noel for his help in preparing the appendix on meditation.

49 If you are happy with your own way of praying you may not need any of the forms of meditation. Ultimately, each person discovers his or her own way of praying: 'God carries each person along a different road' – St John of the Cross, *Living Flame of Love*.

50 John Main, *Word into Silence*, DLT, 1980, Paulist, 1981, p. 9, 53.

51 Louis Hughes OP, *The Art of Allowing*, Columba Press, 2010, p. 104 and 106.

52 M. Basil Pennington, *Daily We Touch Him*, Image Books, New York, 1979, p. 71.

53 *The Way of a Pilgrim*, trans. R. M. French, Ballintine Books, New York, 1994, p. 7.